AF395483

THE HIDDEN LANGUAGE OF FLOWERS
A BOTANICAL STROLL THROUGH THE PRADO

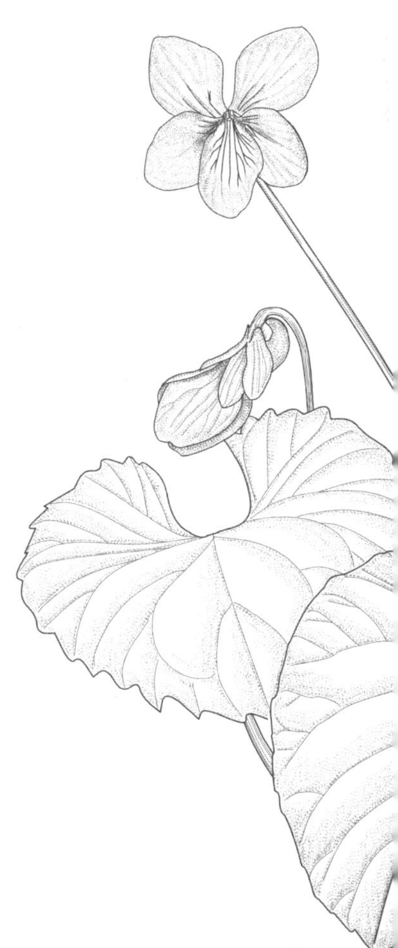

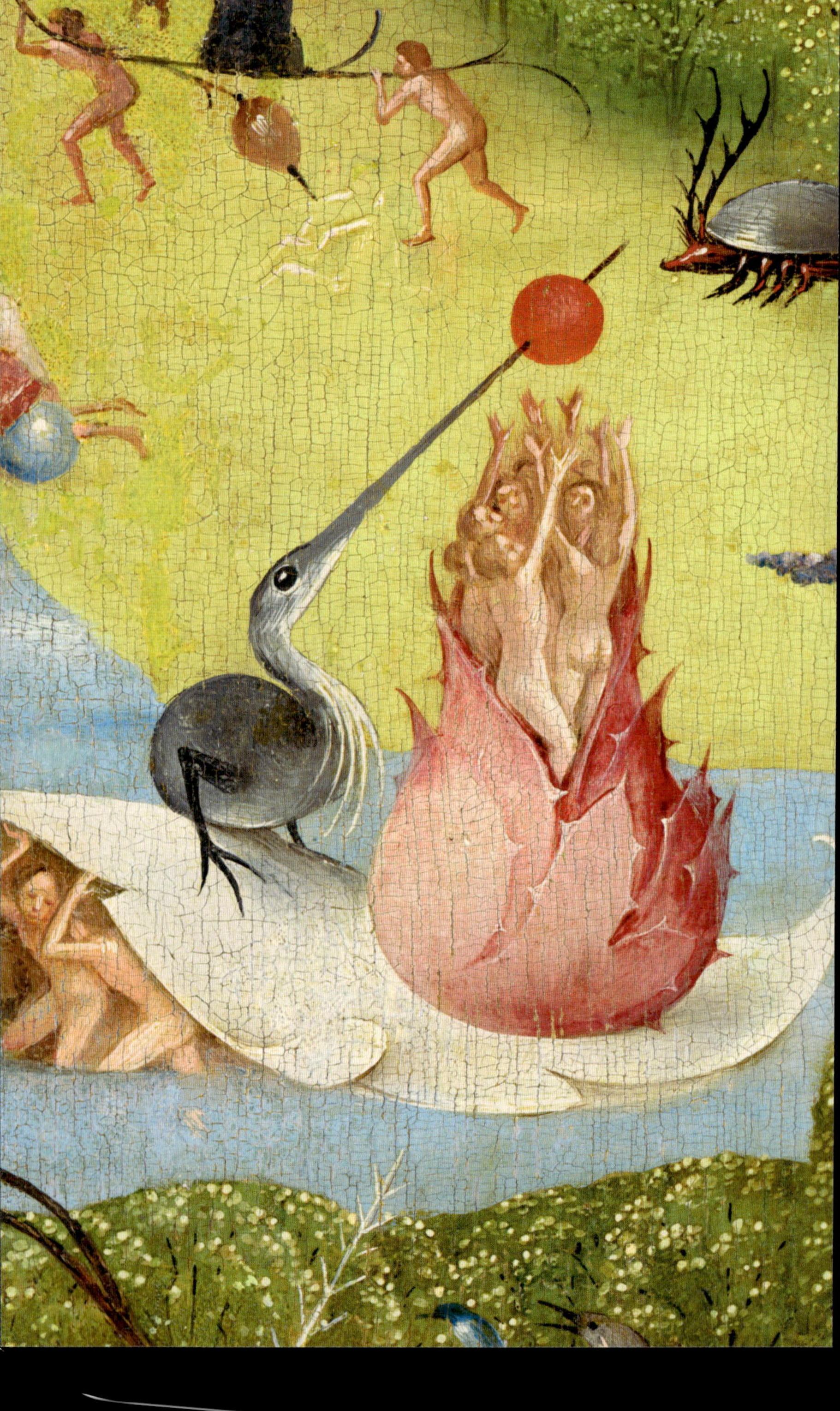

THE HIDDEN LANGUAGE OF FLOWERS

A BOTANICAL STROLL THROUGH THE PRADO

Eduardo Barba Gómez

MUSEO NACIONAL DEL PRADO

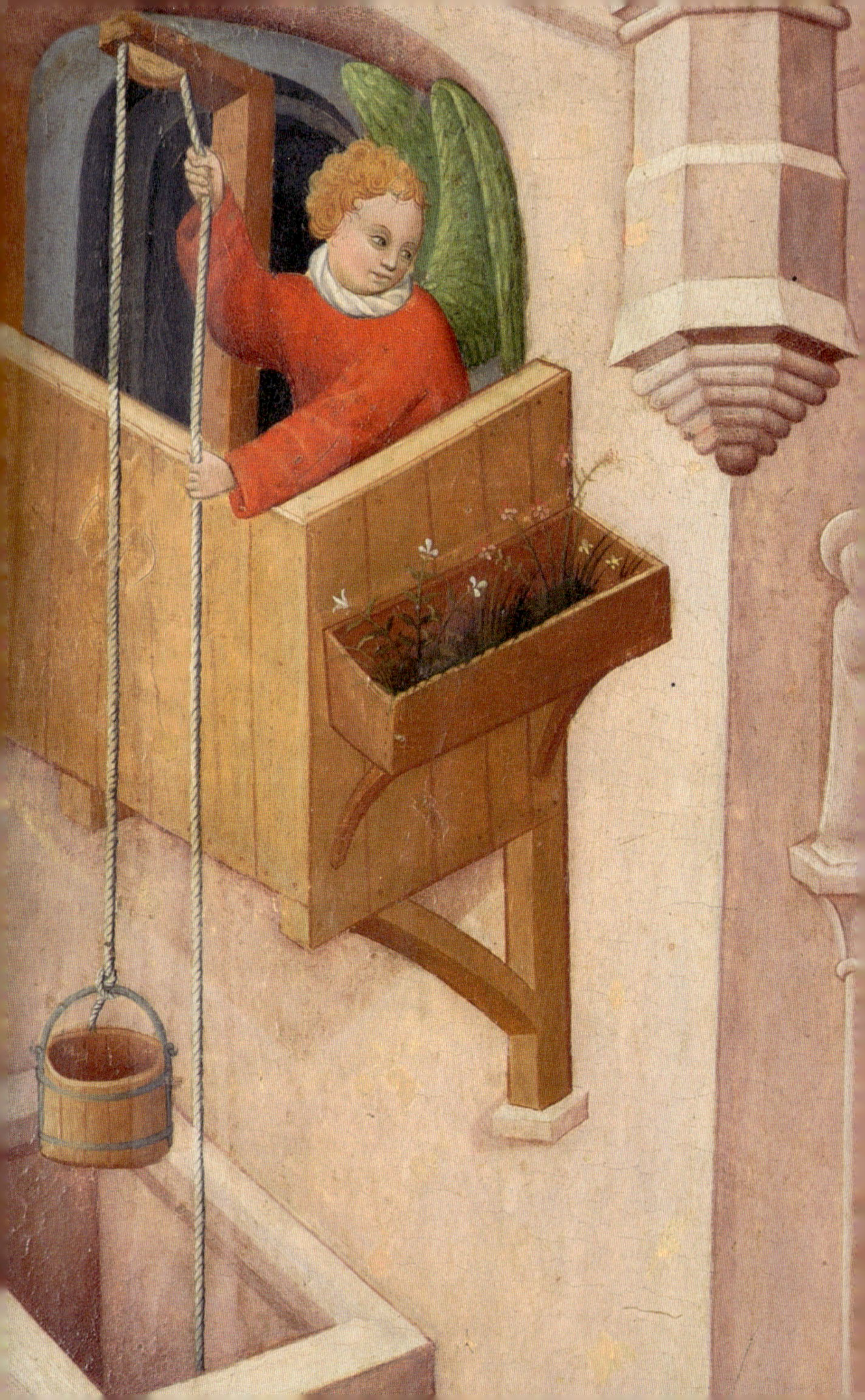

Many works of art are brimming with vibrant plant life, while in others, flora is woven more subtly into the tapestry. Yet, regardless of its prominence, botany consistently plays a pivotal role in the narratives artists strive to convey. Flowers may serve as emblems of a subject's lineage, leaves embody profound emotions, and trees infuse scenes with their innate symbolism.

Artists of the past possessed a remarkable ability for observing the natural world. They meticulously rendered plants as integral characters, not mere background elements. Familiar species often shared the canvas with exotic specimens hailing from distant lands.

Sadly, modern society has largely lost this profound connection to the plant kingdom, a disconnect mirrored even in how we engage with art. Yet, even the humblest leaf or blossom can unlock a trove of information about a work's mythological, religious, sociopolitical, or cultural significance. Every petal whispers a story; we need only to seek out the next flower and listen to its tale to feel a kinship with the artists, like gardeners strolling through the halls of the Museo del Prado.

Eduardo Barba Gómez

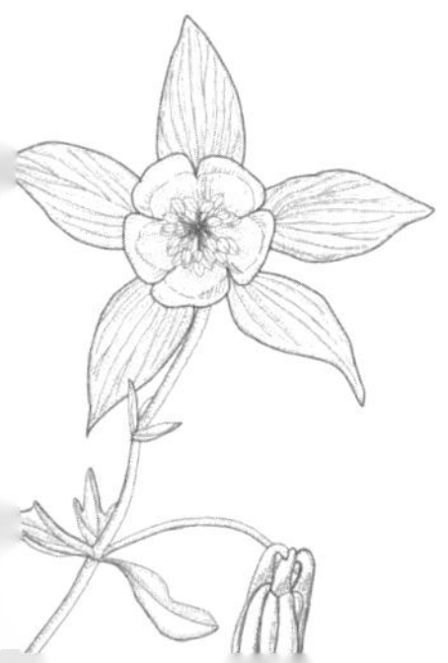

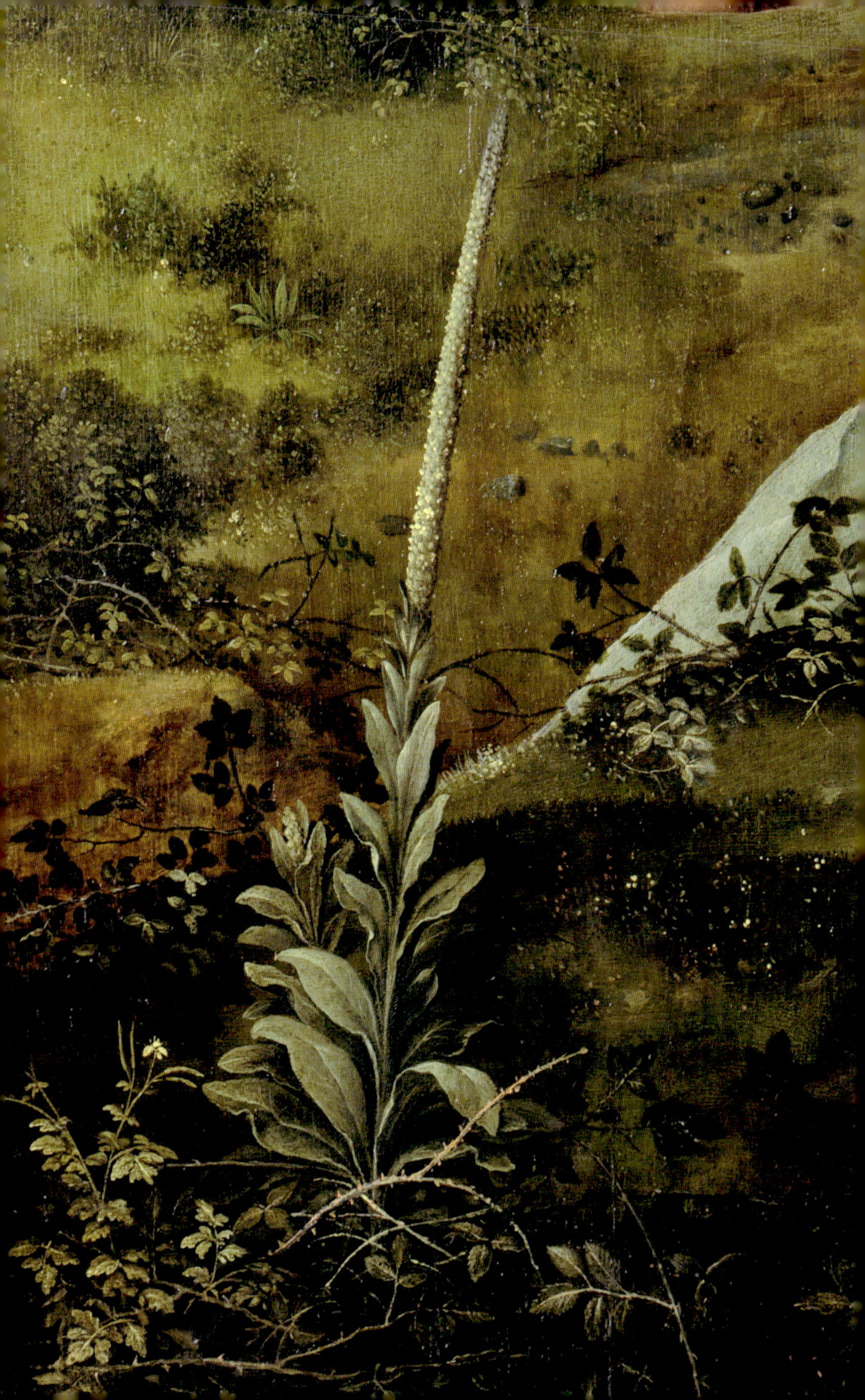

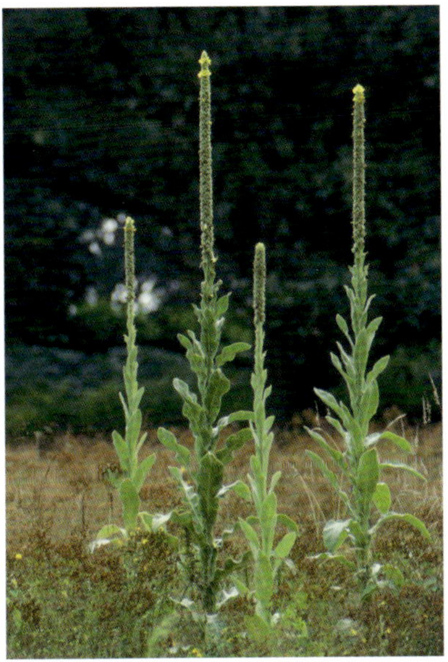

GREAT MULLEIN

This landscape depicts a natural setting in present-day Belgium. Many of the plant species shown, almost like characters in the painting, have a marked symbolic significance. One very clear example is the grapevine (*Vitis vinifera*) climbing the apple tree (*Malus domestica*) in the foreground: the blood of Christ washing away original sin. On the left, there is a great mullein. Its flowering stem was set alight in ceremonies, including funerals, alluding – as here – to Jesus' death and to the light he brings to the world.

Verbascum thapsus

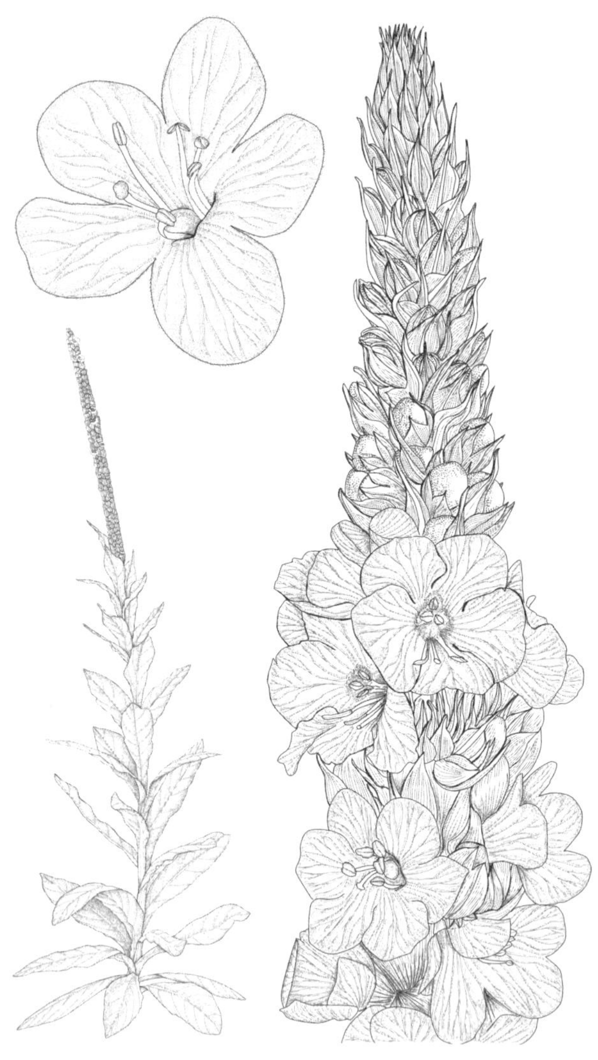

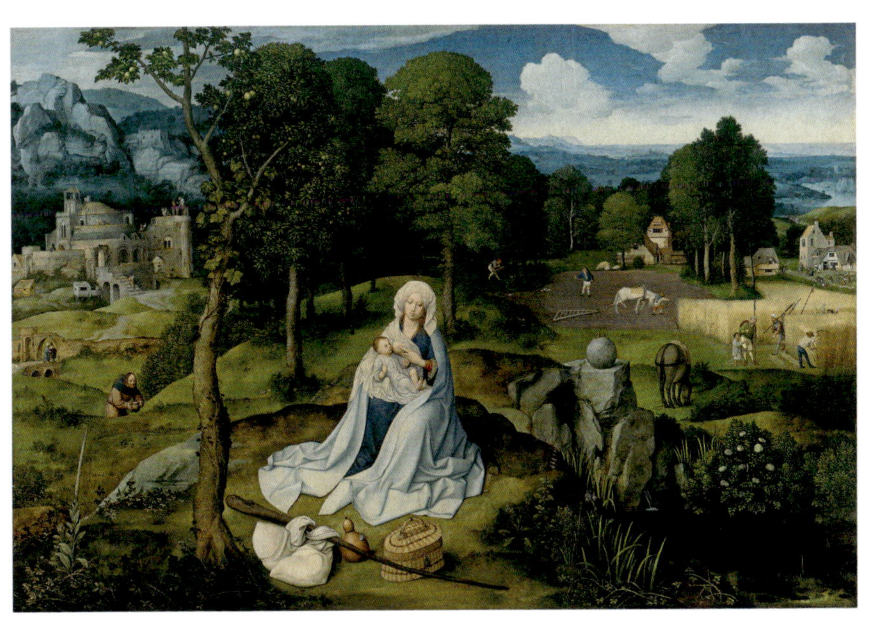

Joachim Patinir
Rest on the Flight into Egypt
1518-1520

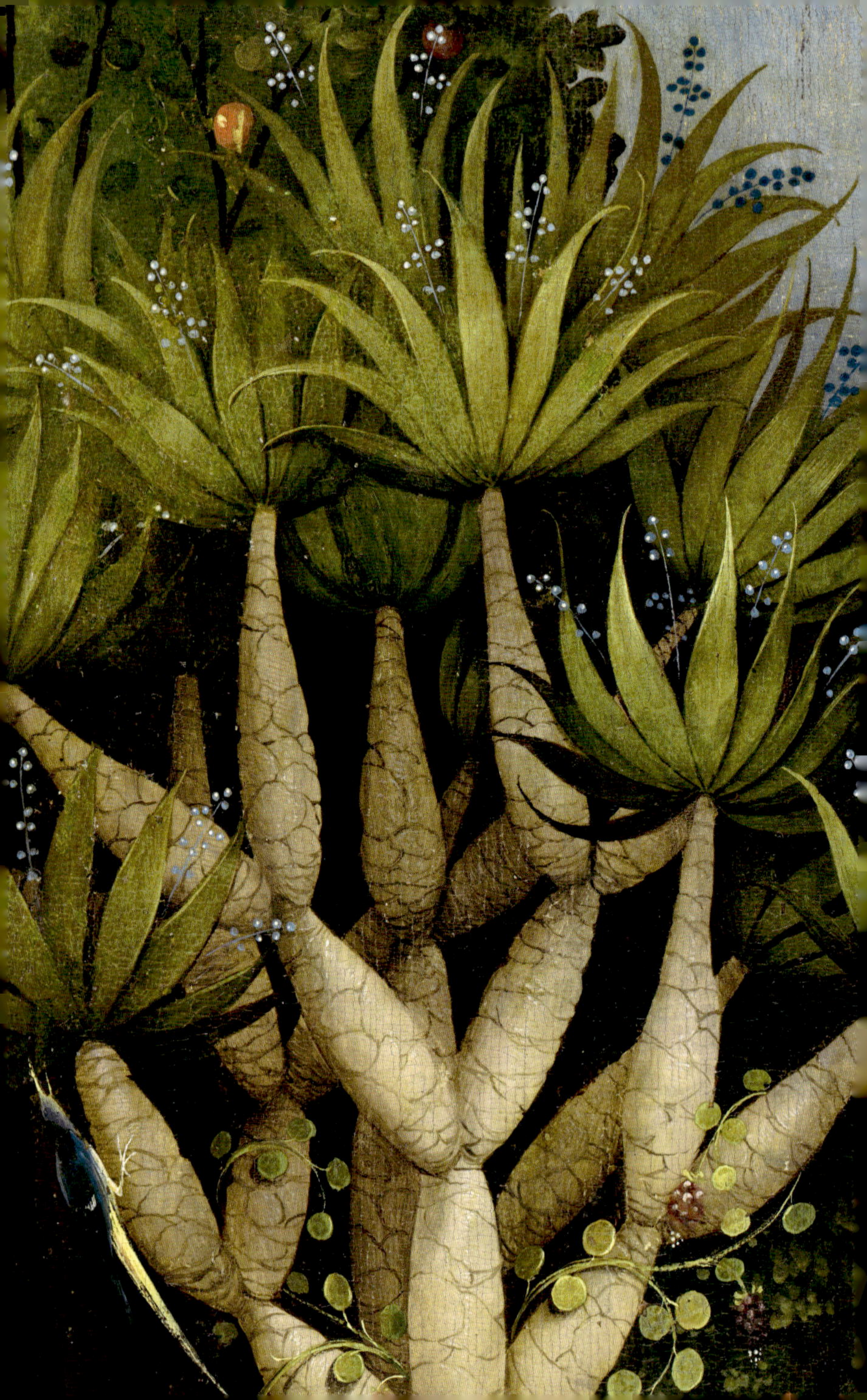

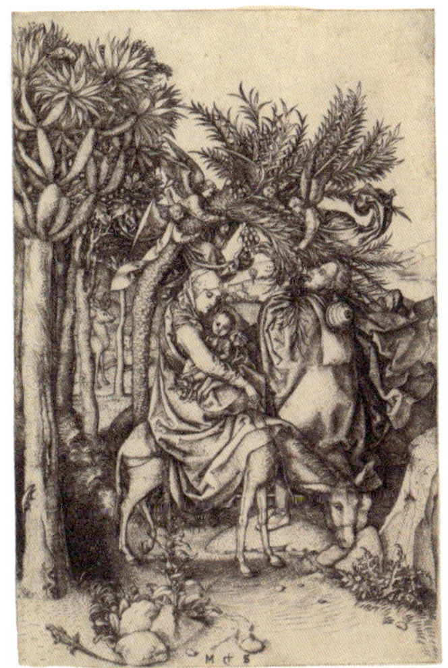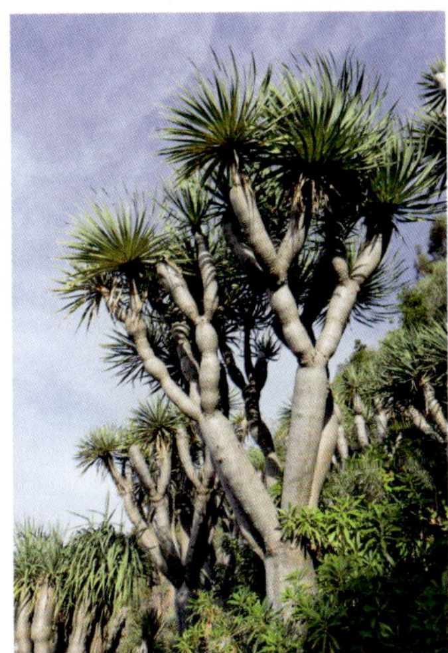

DRAGON TREE

This plant, whose red sap was known as "dragon's blood", was greatly sought after in Europe both for its medicinal properties and as a dye; its popularity almost led to its extinction. It is mainly native to Tenerife, one of the Canary Islands. Sugar was exported from there to northern Europe, which is how local artists found out about the dragon tree. Bosch is thought to have seen this plant in prints, for example by Martin Schongauer (c. 1470), or in the incunabulum *Liber Chronicarum* (1493), illustrated by Michael Wolgemut. Behind the dragon tree there is a veritable orchard of apple trees (*Malus domestica*) laden with red fruit.

Dracaena draco

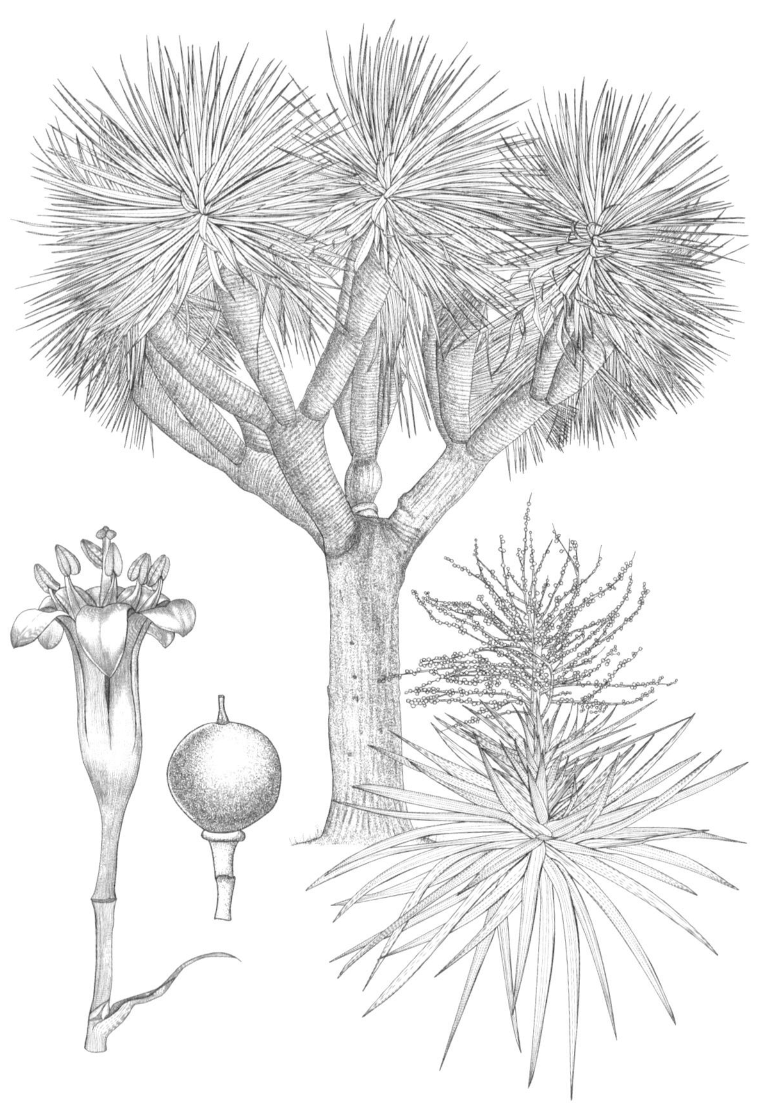

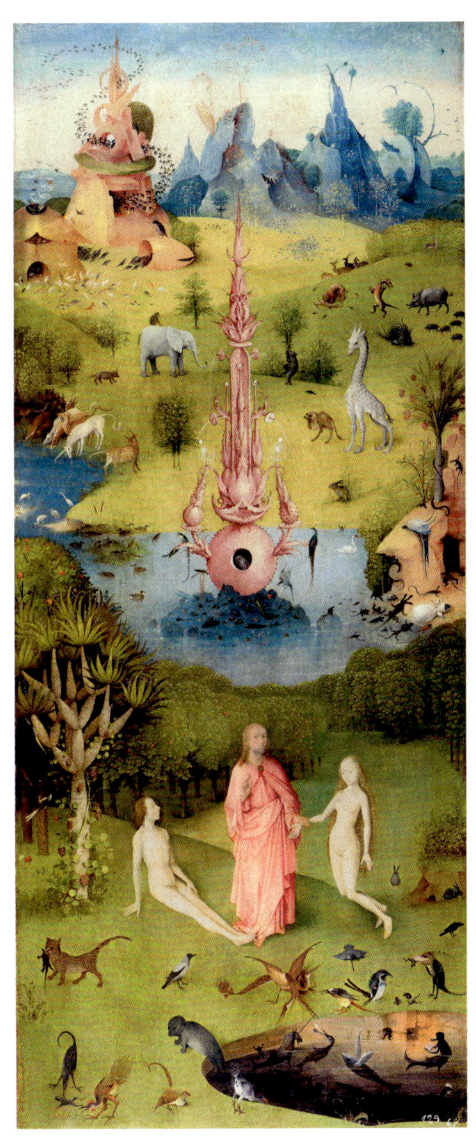

Hieronymus Bosch
The Garden of Earthly Delights Triptych (left panel)
1490-1500

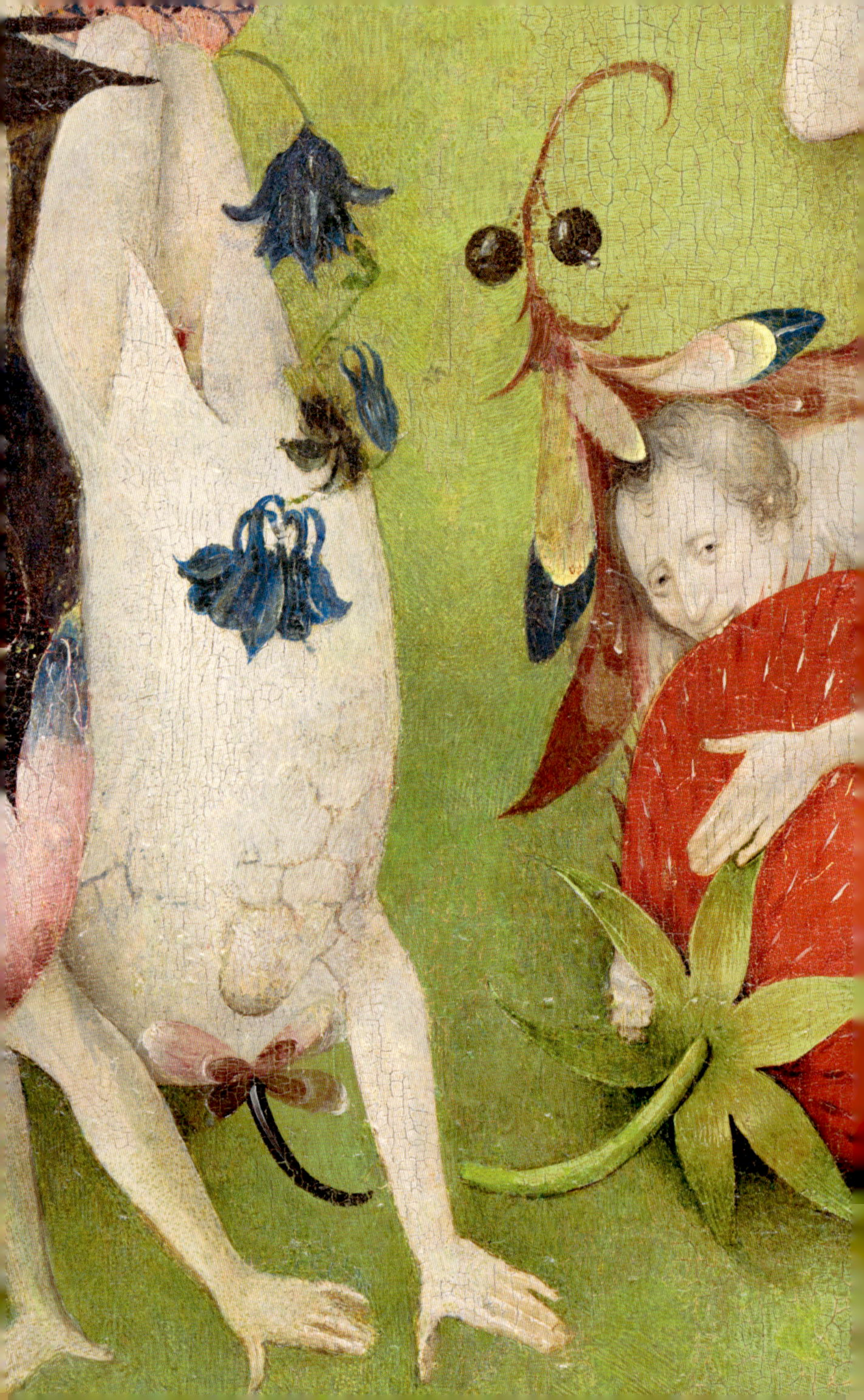

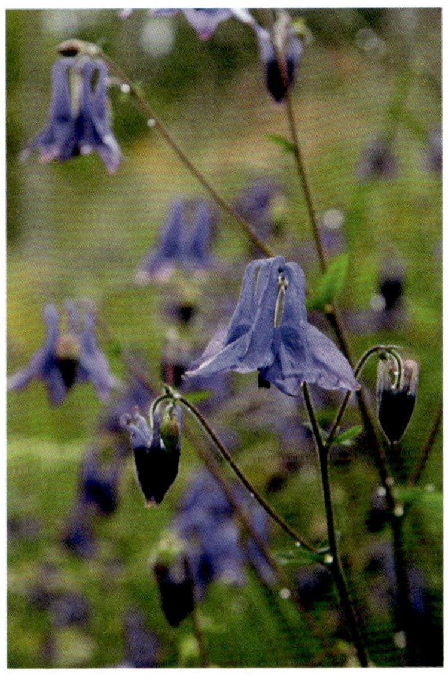

COLUMBINE

In their amazing shape, these flowers resemble eagles' talons or doves in flight. The species was widely grown in medieval gardens, not just for its unusually beautiful flowers but also because its seeds and roots – though poisonous – were used to make aphrodisiac medicines. To the right of the columbine is a strawberry (*Fragaria vesca*) of grotesque proportions. The strawberry – which recurs elsewhere in the central panel – was a symbol of the sensual pleasures; like them, strawberries never satiate man's hunger, no matter how many he may eat.

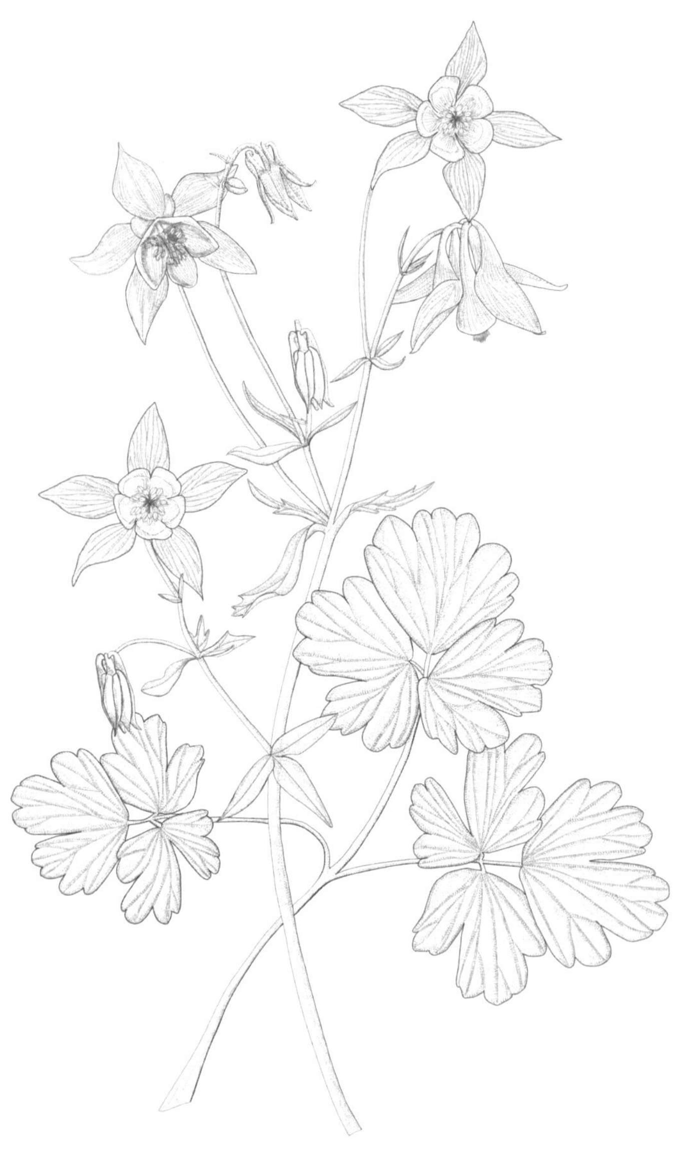

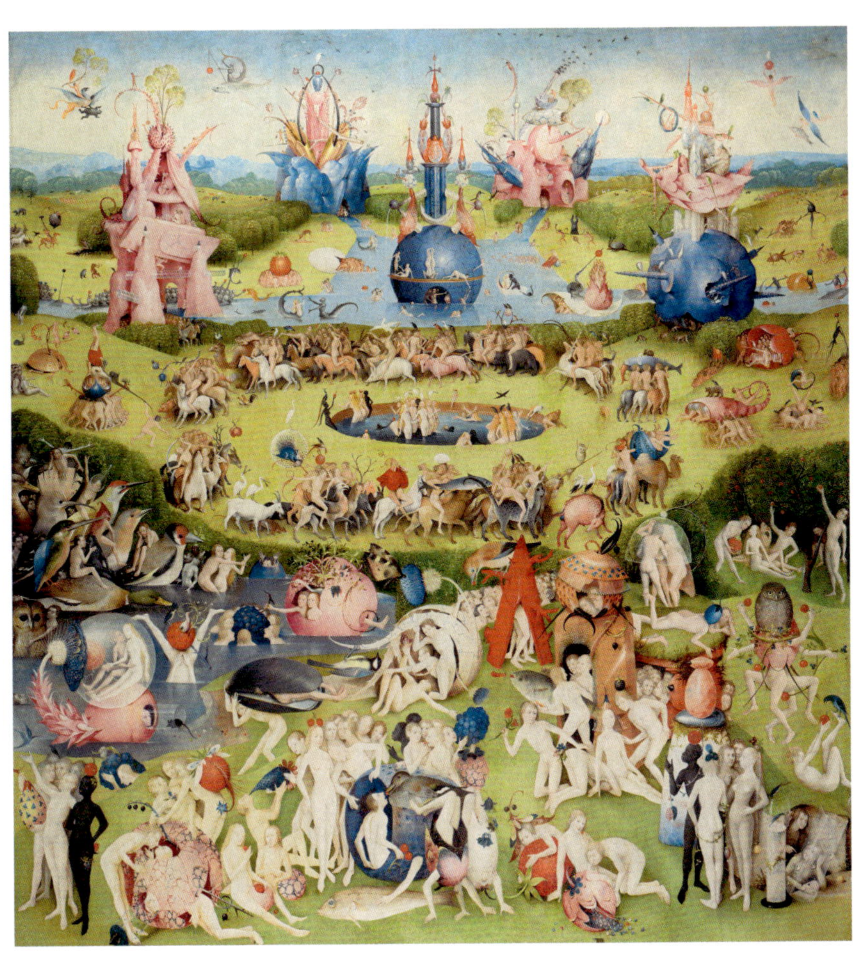

Hieronymus Bosch
The Garden of Earthly Delights Triptych (central panel)
1490-1500

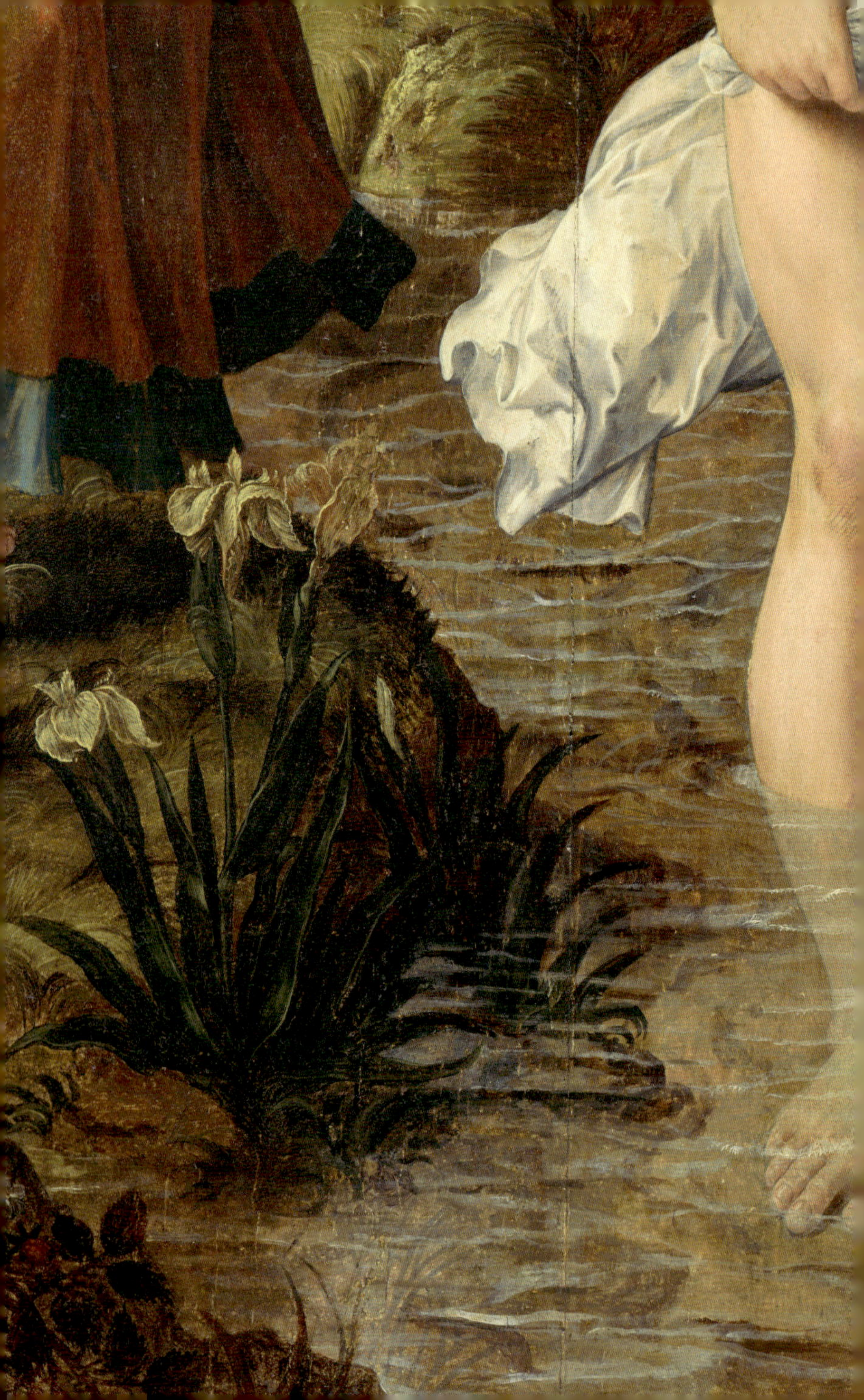

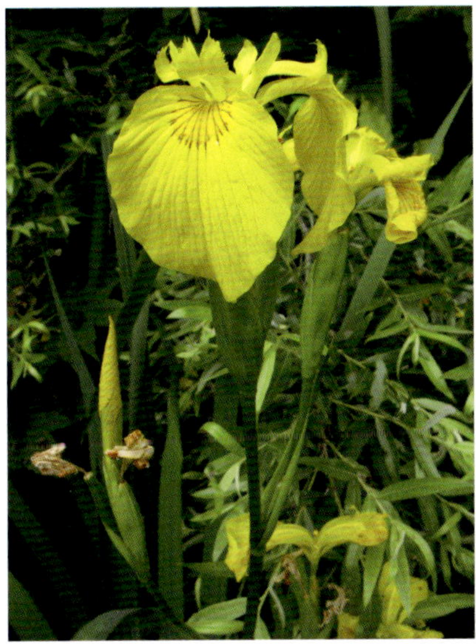

YELLOW IRIS

The yellow iris is a species that grows near water, for example on the banks of rivers, streams or ponds. In this landscape, two clumps of yellow iris are visible beside Jesus. Because of its sword-shaped leaves, its presence in paintings is sometimes associated with the suffering that pierces the heart of the Virgin Mary. As a symbol of the Incarnation of Christ, it is sometimes found in Annunciation scenes. Its Greek name, *Iris*, in use since ancient times, means 'rainbow', a reference to the different colours of its flowers.

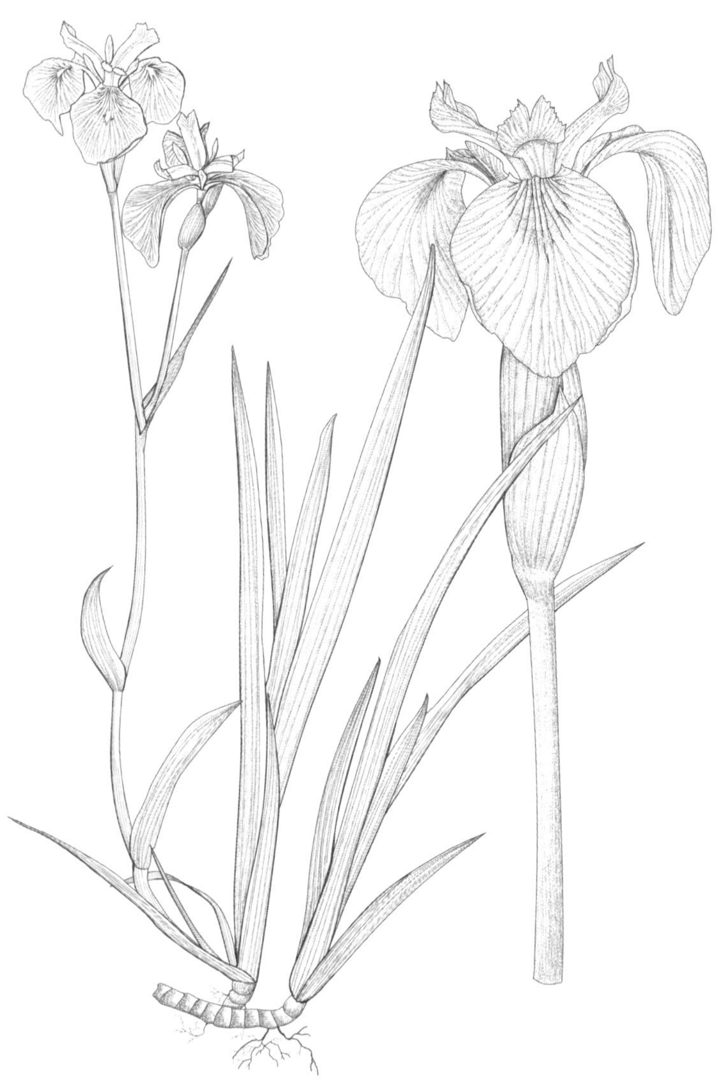

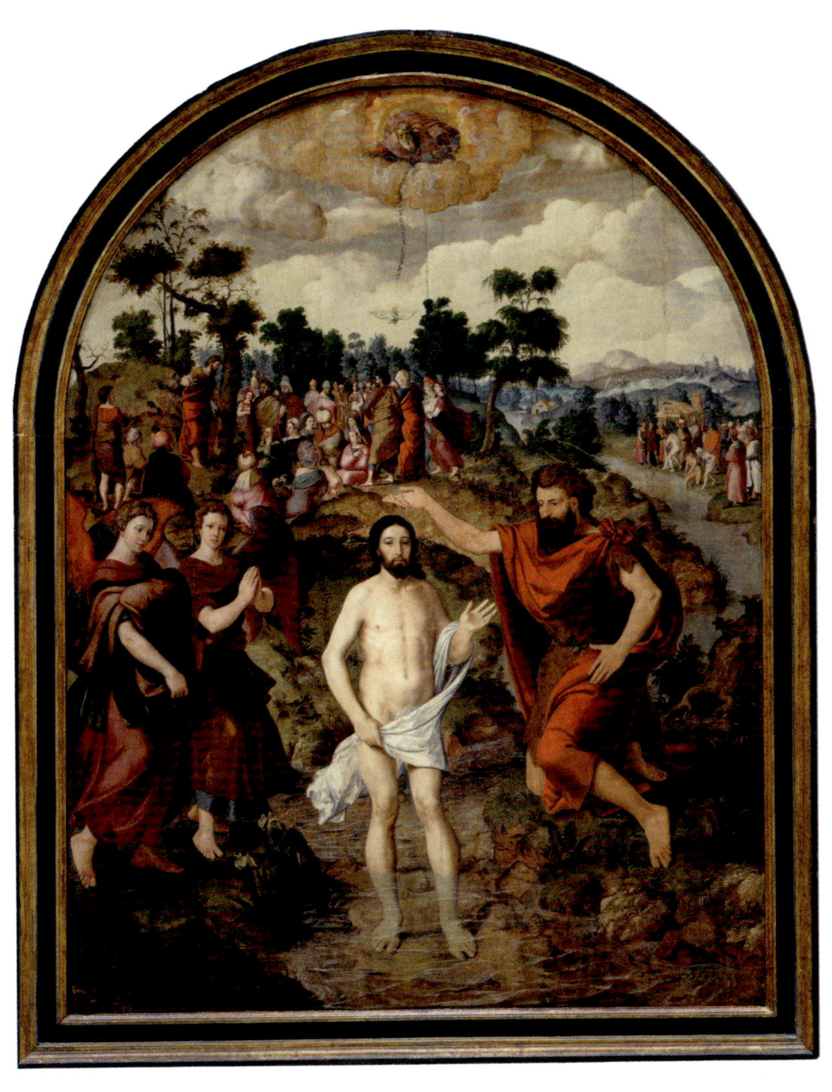

Pierre (Pieter Jansz.) Pourbus the Elder
Triptych of Saints John the Baptist and John the Evangelist (central panel)
1549

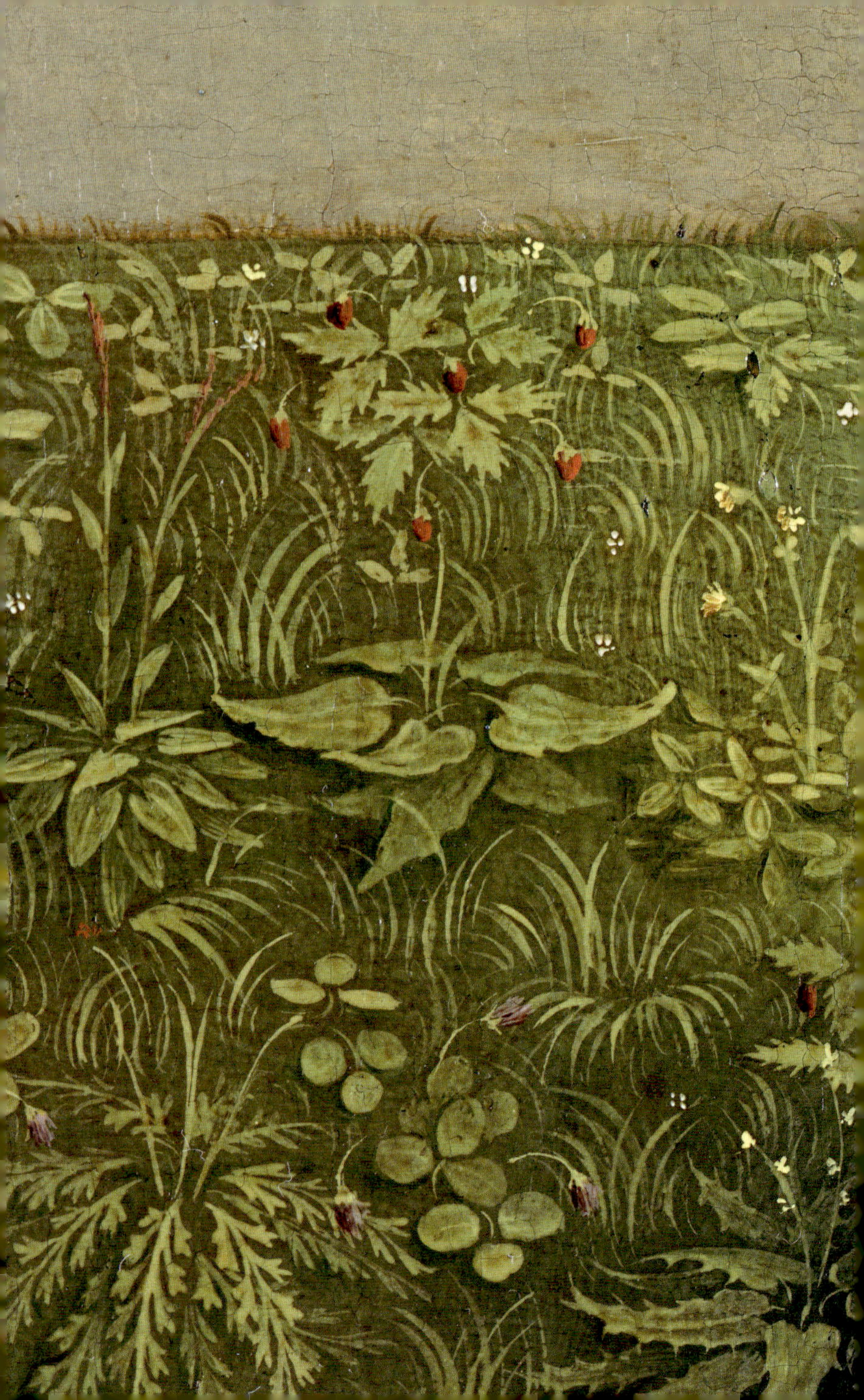

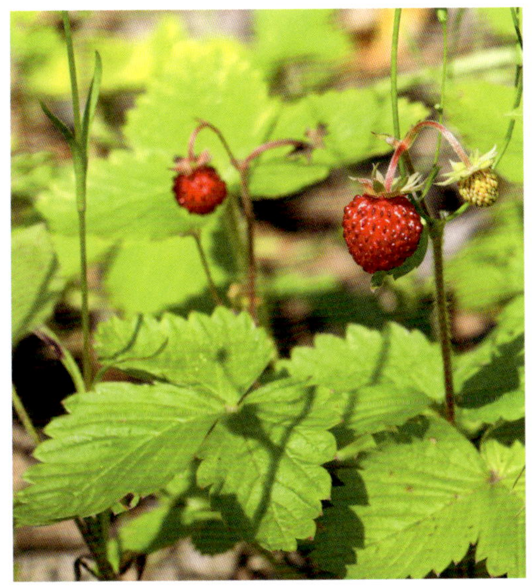

WILD STRAWBERRY

A wealth of plant species can be found in this painting, not only on the meadow-like terrace where the musician angels are playing, but also in the carved decorations on capitals, bases and other architectural elements, as well as in the gold tracery and floral motifs adorning the fabrics. The meadow contains around twenty different species, of which the most abundant is the strawberry, some of whose symbolic associations date back to classical antiquity, when it epitomised paradise. Its red fruits also represent the blood shed by Christ in his martyrdom, while its trefoil leaves symbolise the Holy Trinity.

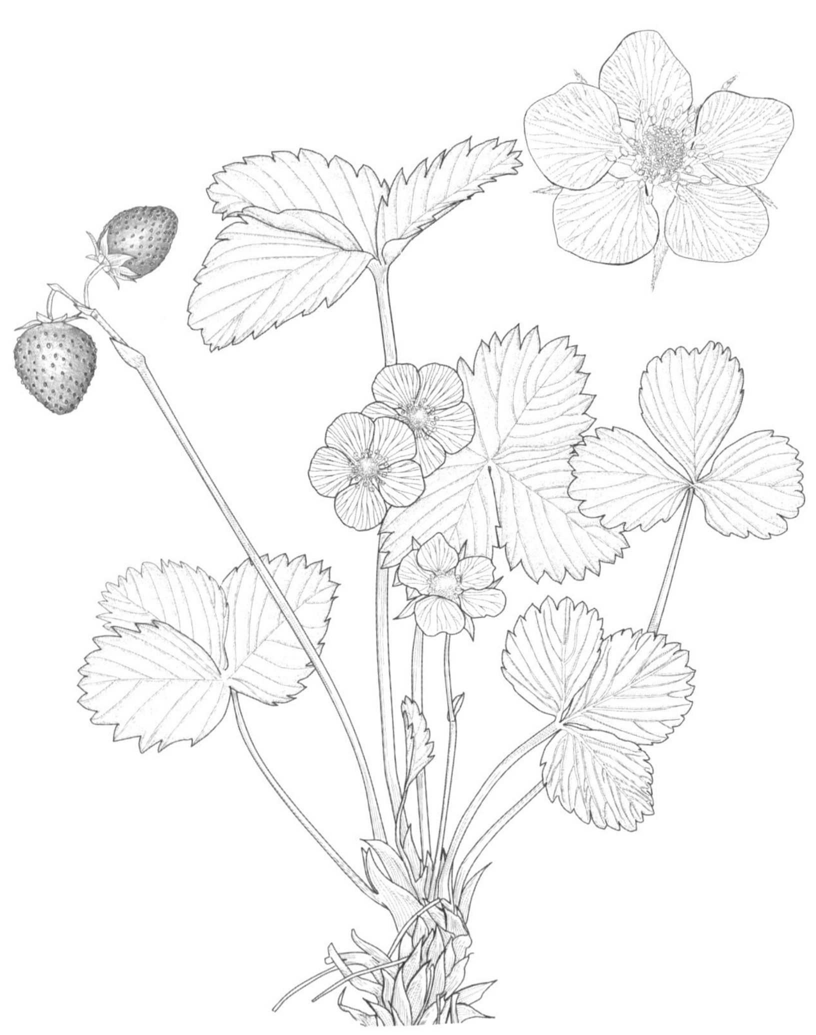

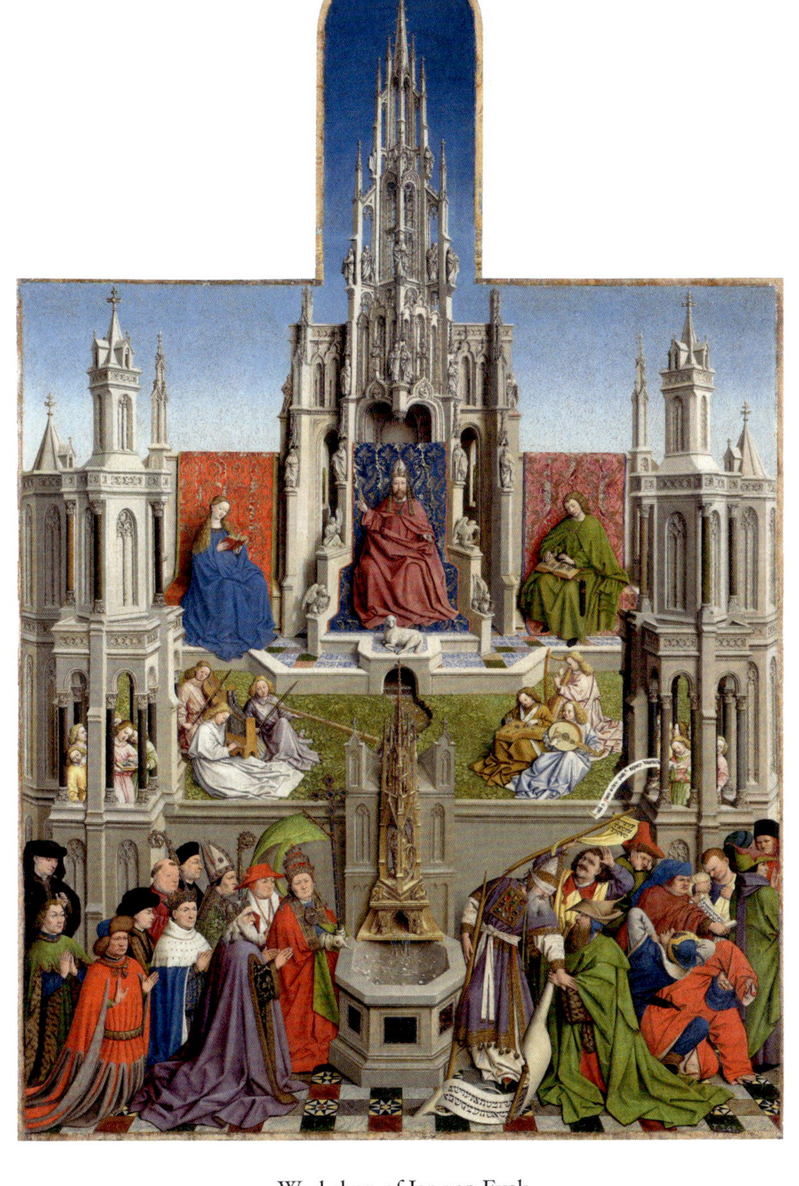

Workshop of Jan van Eyck
The Fountain of Grace
1440–1450

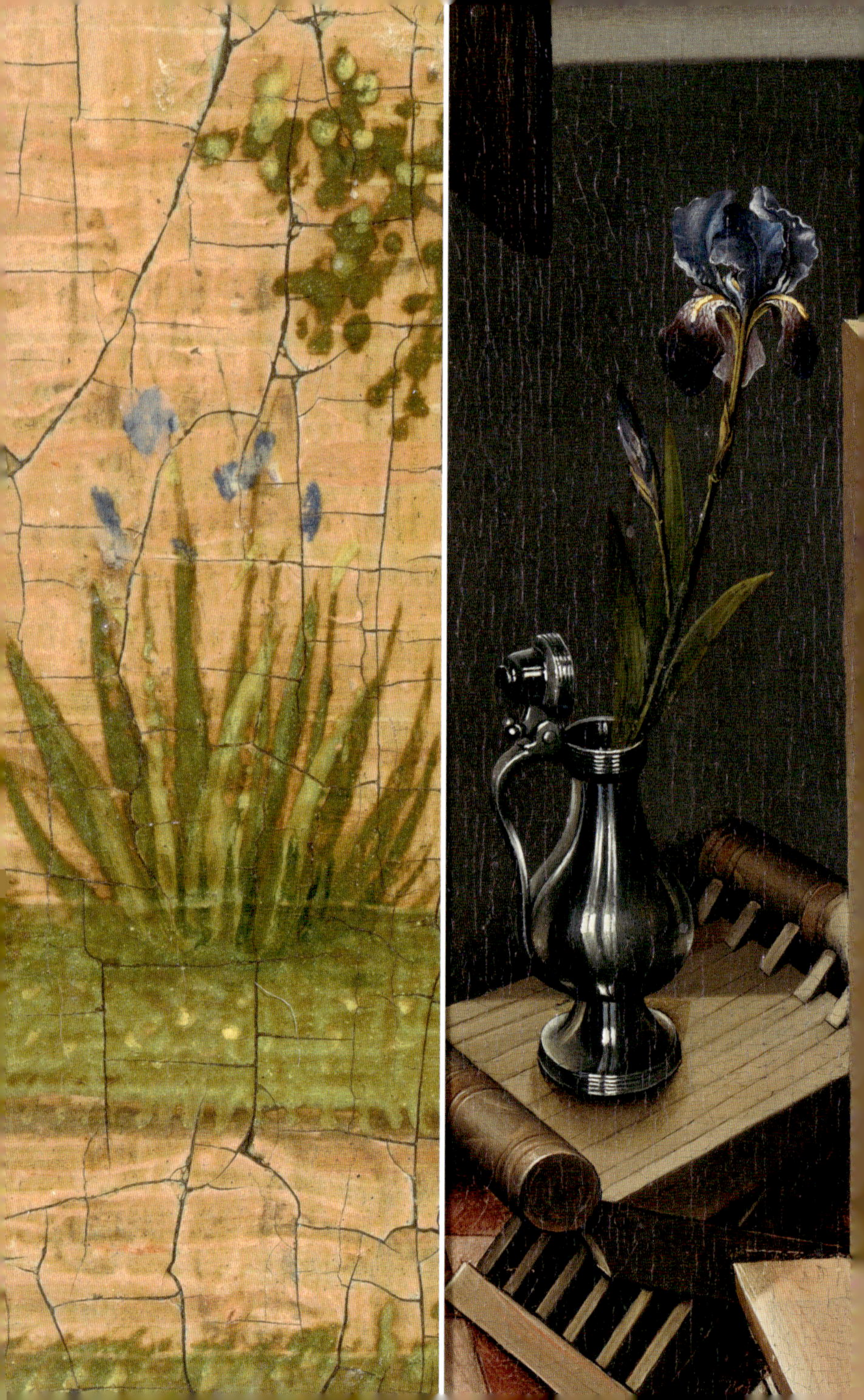

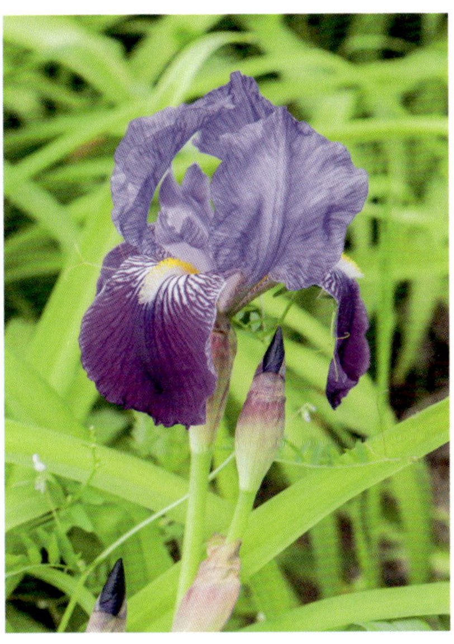

BEARDED IRIS

These two panels belong to a dismembered triptych. The central panel was lost, but the two outer paintings are still linked by botany. In the right-hand panel, Saint Barbara sits patiently reading beside a delicate iris stem in a small pewter vase. Its open flower displays the yellow "beard" so characteristic of this plant. In the left-hand panel, against the crenellated garden wall, there is a tiny clump of irises with four flowers, from which the iris adorning Saint Barbara's room must have been cut.

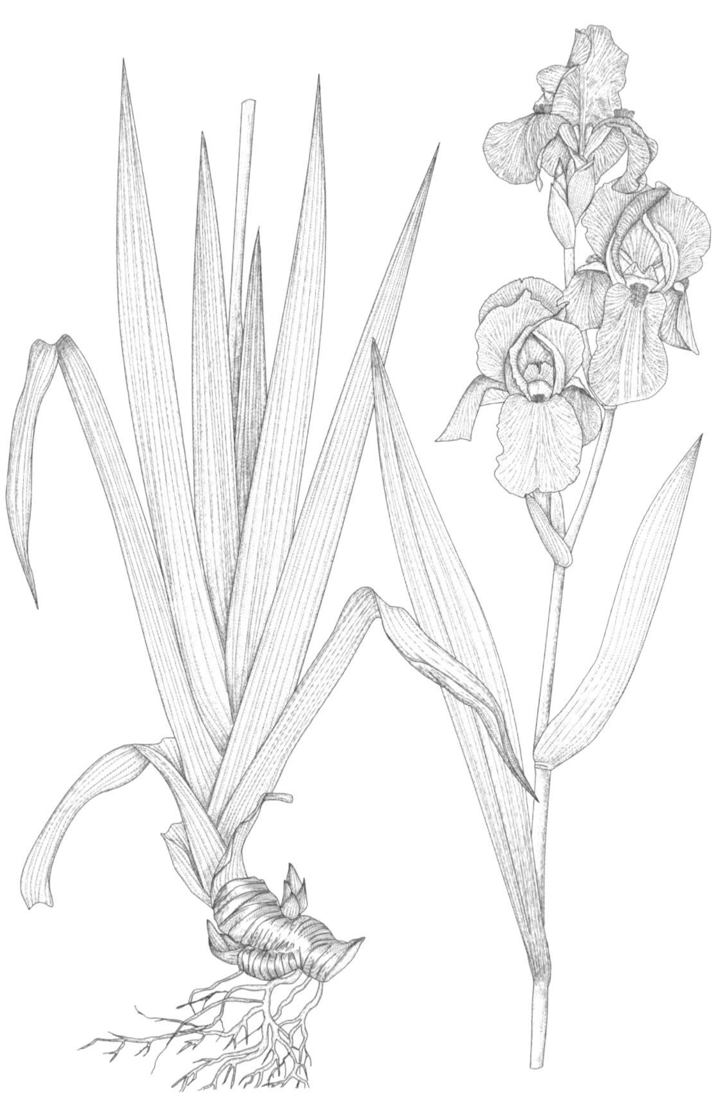

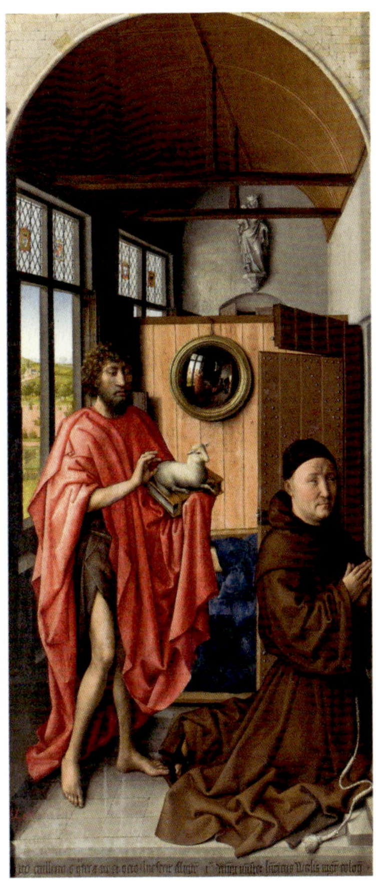 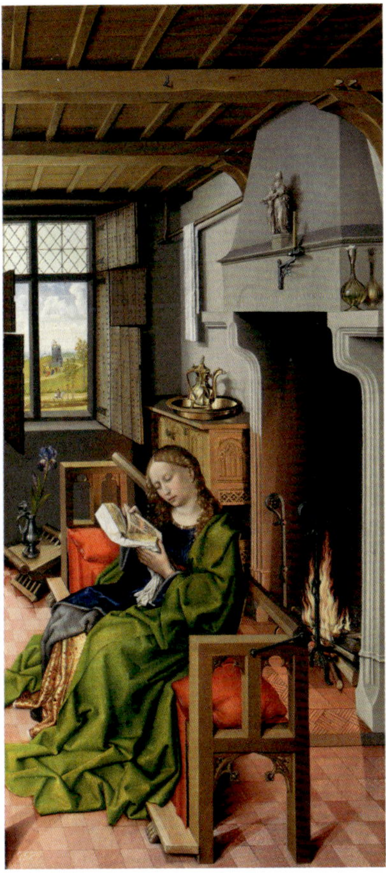

Follower of the Master of Flémalle
Heinrich von Werl with Saint John the Baptist /
Saint Barbara
1438

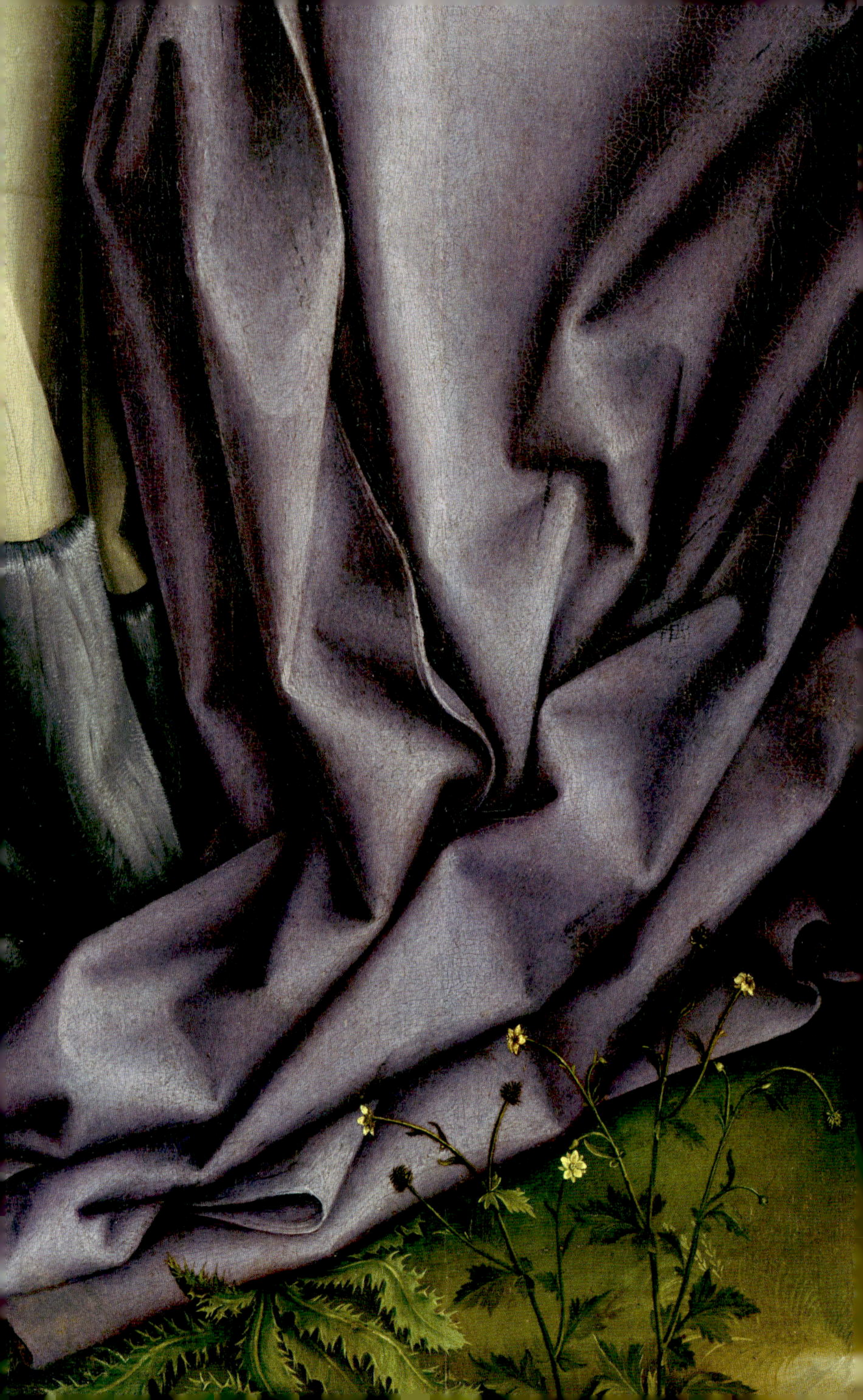

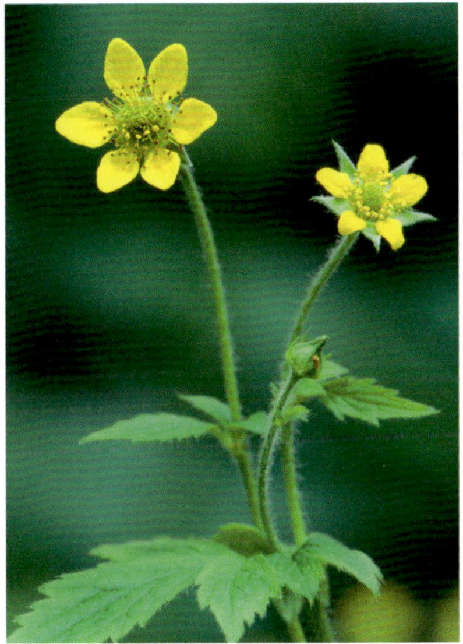

WOOD AVENS

In ancient times, many plants were grown for their protective properties. The German herbarium *Garden of Health* (*Gart der Gesundheit*, 1485), recommended planting wood avens in the garden, since the scent given off by the roots repels venomous animals. The 12th-century physician Matthaeus Platearius claimed that the devil himself could not harm a house where this root was to be found. Van der Weyden's masterly depiction of this herb perfectly captures its small, five-petalled flowers and its hook-covered fruits, which can easily cling to animals' fur, thus helping to spread the species far from the mother plant.

Geum urbanum

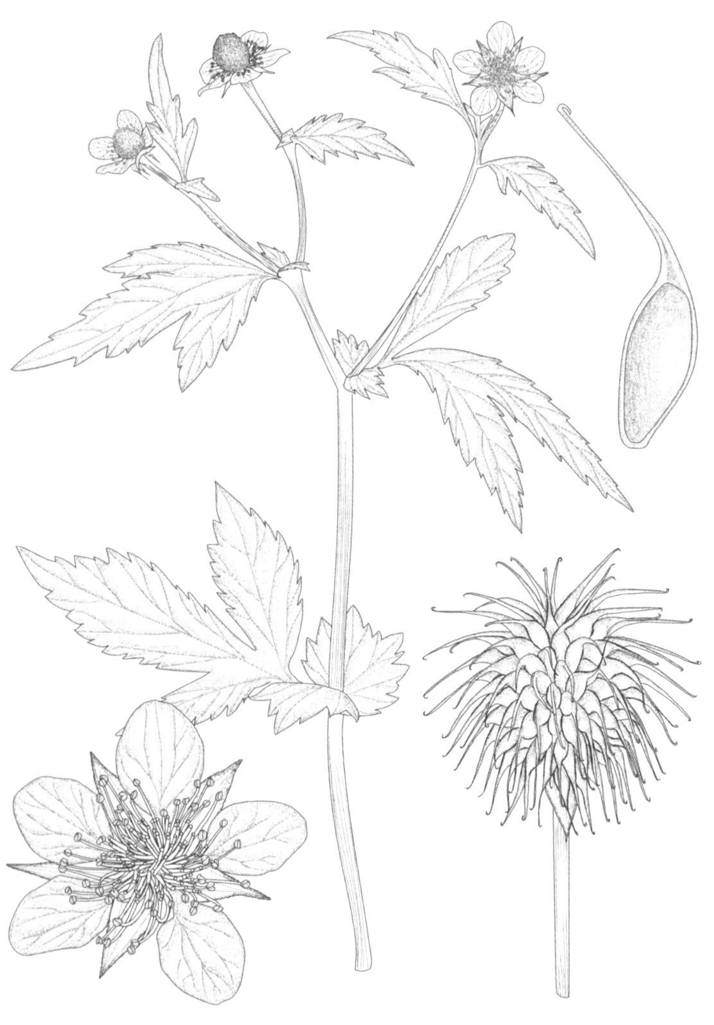

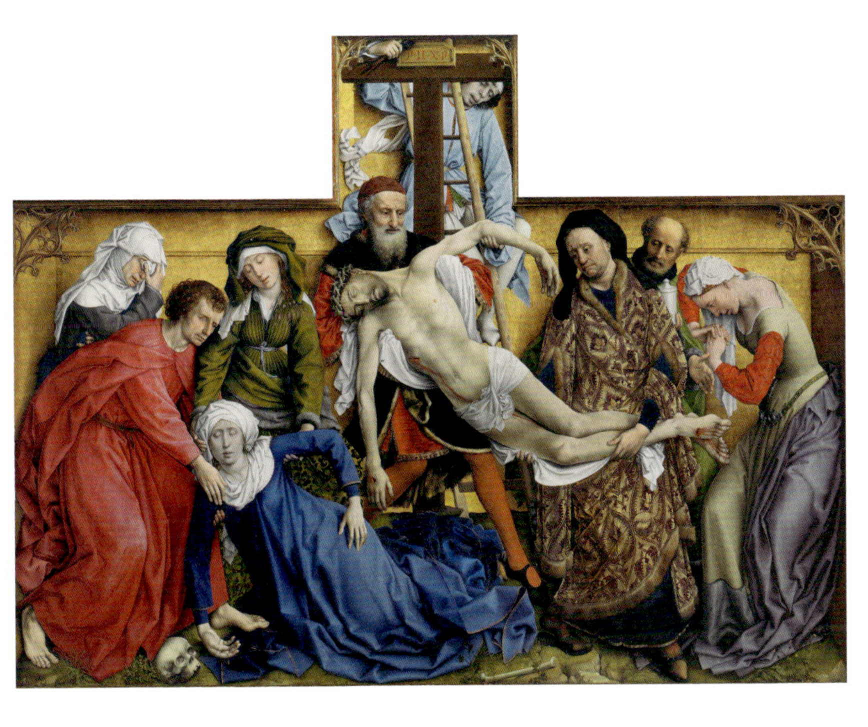

Rogier van der Weyden
The Descent from the Cross
Before 1443

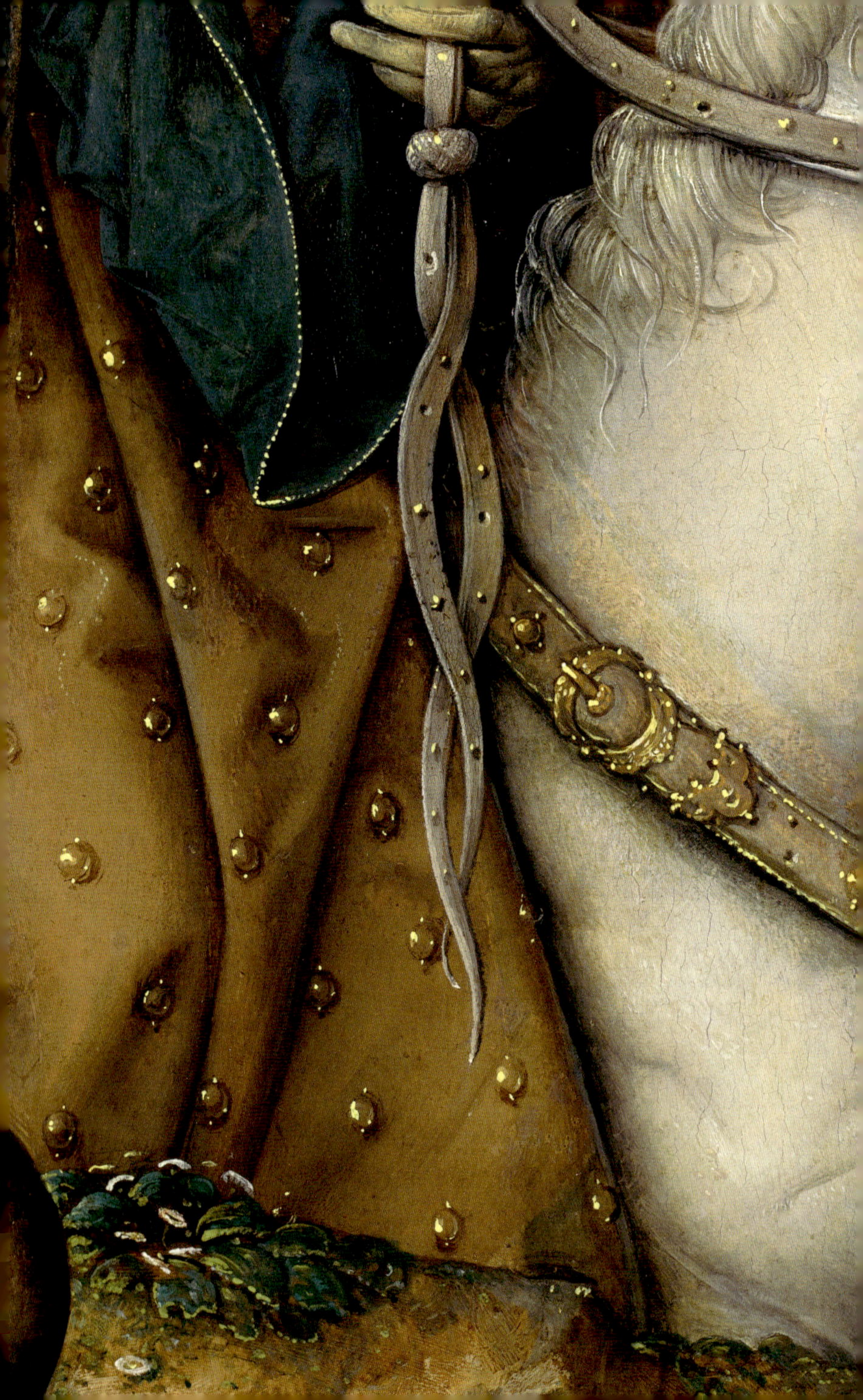

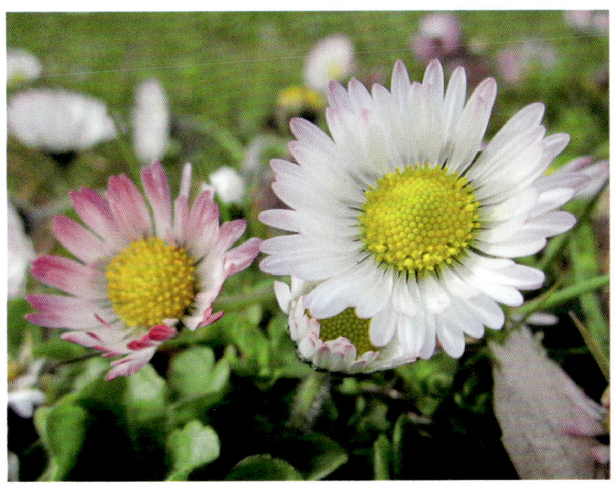

DAISY

The daisy is one of the most common plants in artistic representations of all kinds. It appeared, for example, on the Ishtar gate in Babylon, and was used as an ornamental motif in ancient Rome. Today, because it reproduces easily, it can be seen in lawns and meadows all over the world. Its petals are white, though sometimes with a reddish tinge. In this panel by Juan de Flandes, in fact, the daises just at the foot of the cross were painted red, while the rest were left white. The flower symbolises both resurrection and purity.

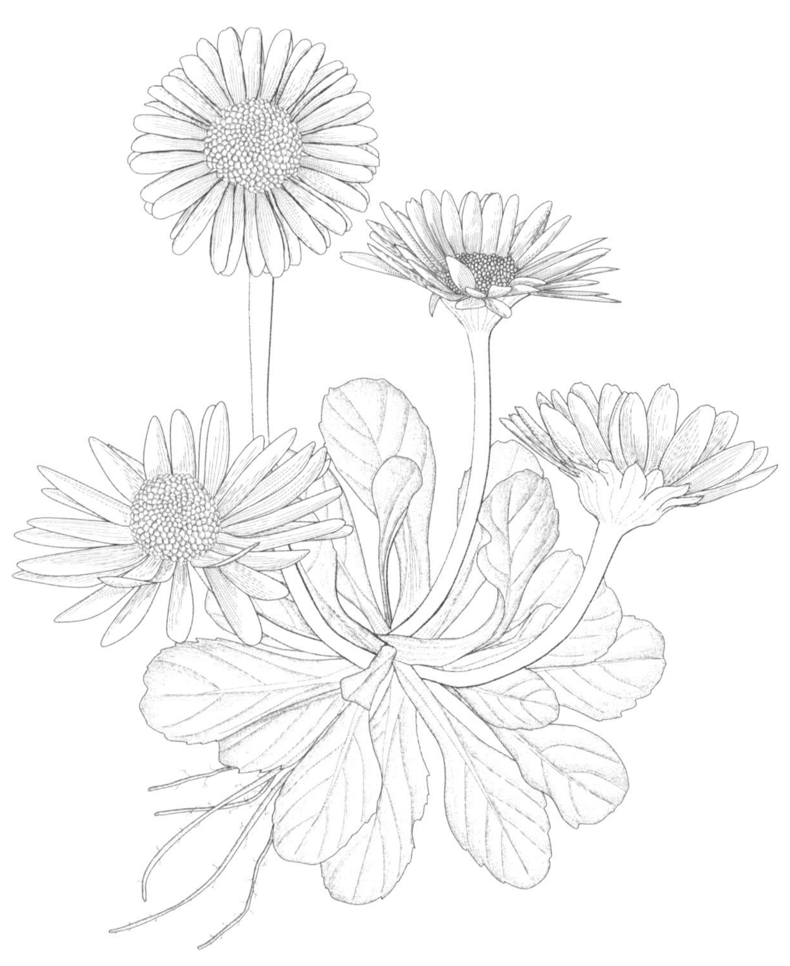

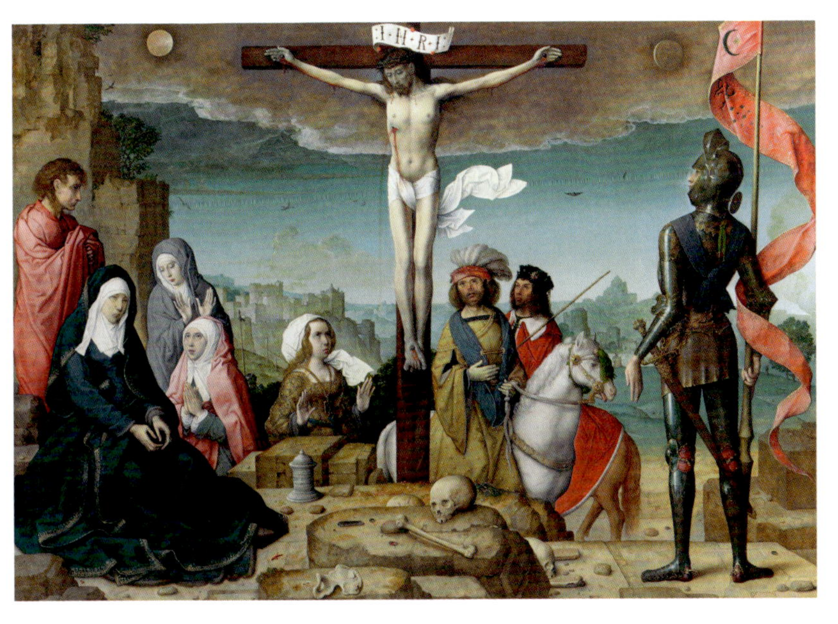

Juan de Flandes
The Crucifixion
1509-1519

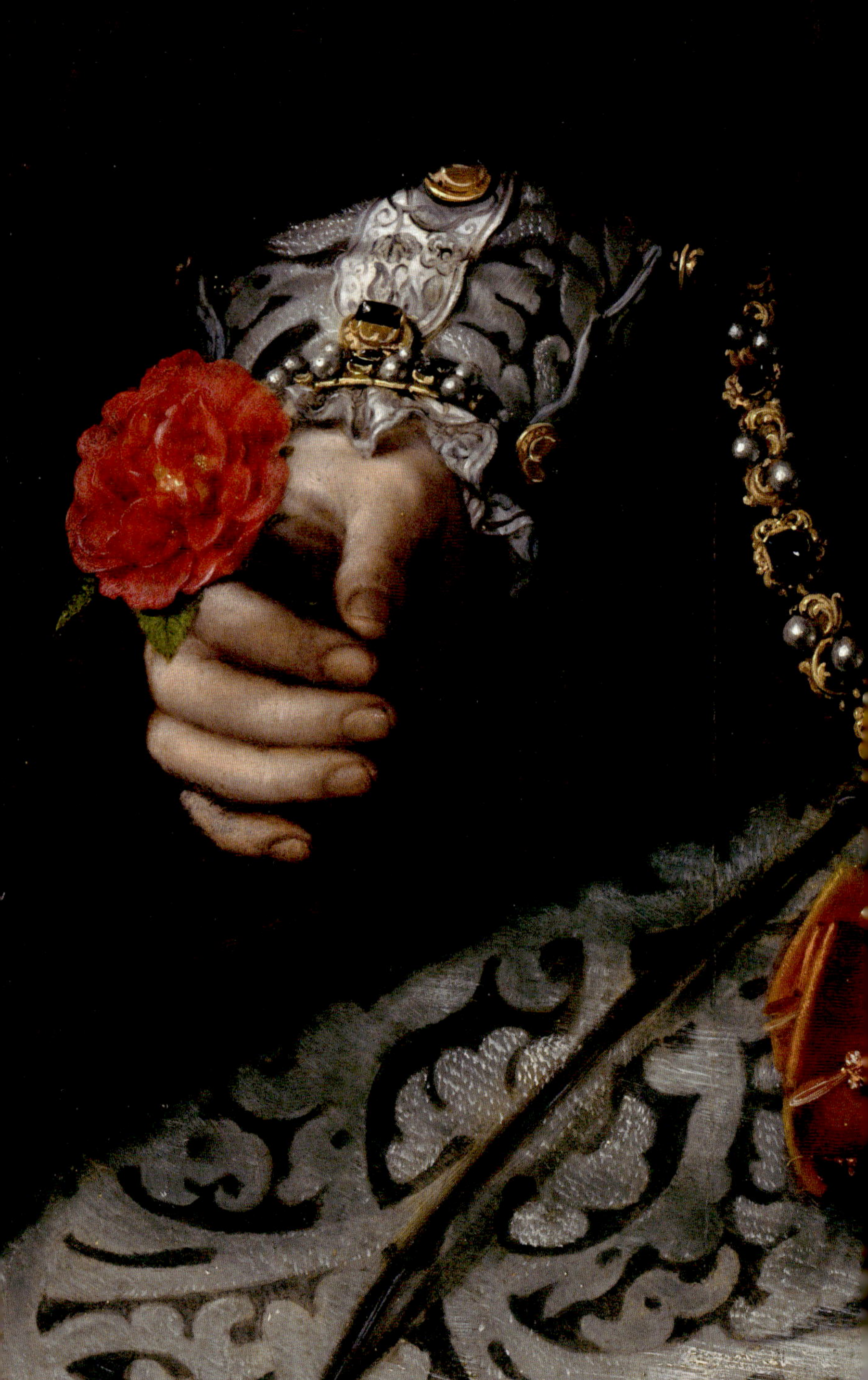

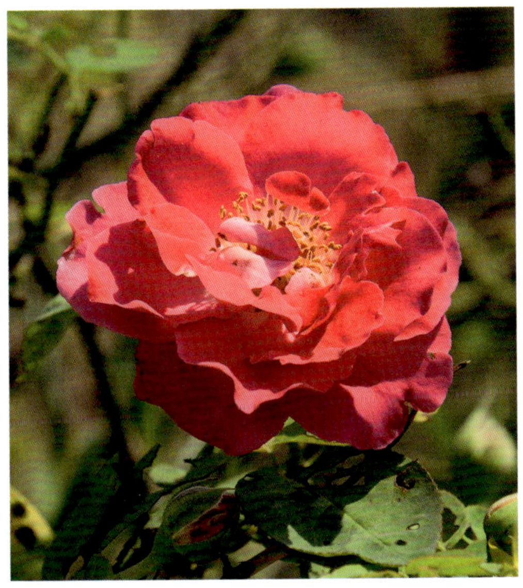

APOTHECARY'S ROSE

The rose is the queen of flowers at the Prado, appearing in hundreds of works of art in the museum's collection. From ancient Egypt to the present day, roses have been cultivated for their beauty and fragrance. In this portrait, Mary Tudor holds an apothecary's rose, the symbol of her noble lineage, the House of Lancaster. This is the most commonly-depicted red rose variety, partly because it is among the most widely grown on account of its countless medicinal properties. Its scent is at once strong and sweet.

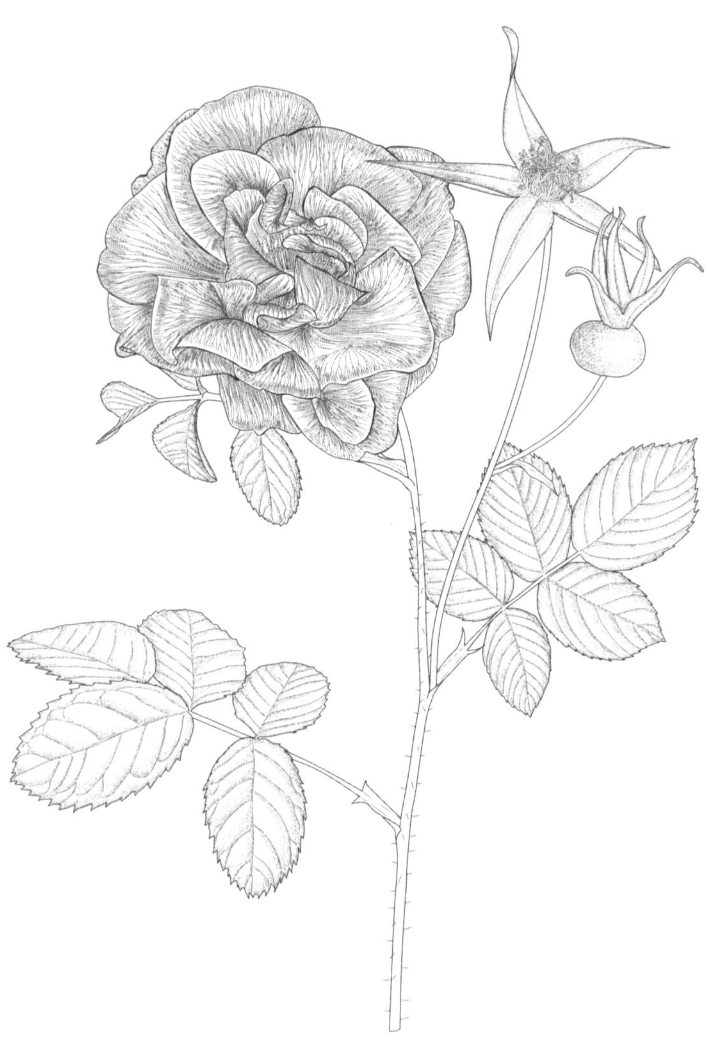

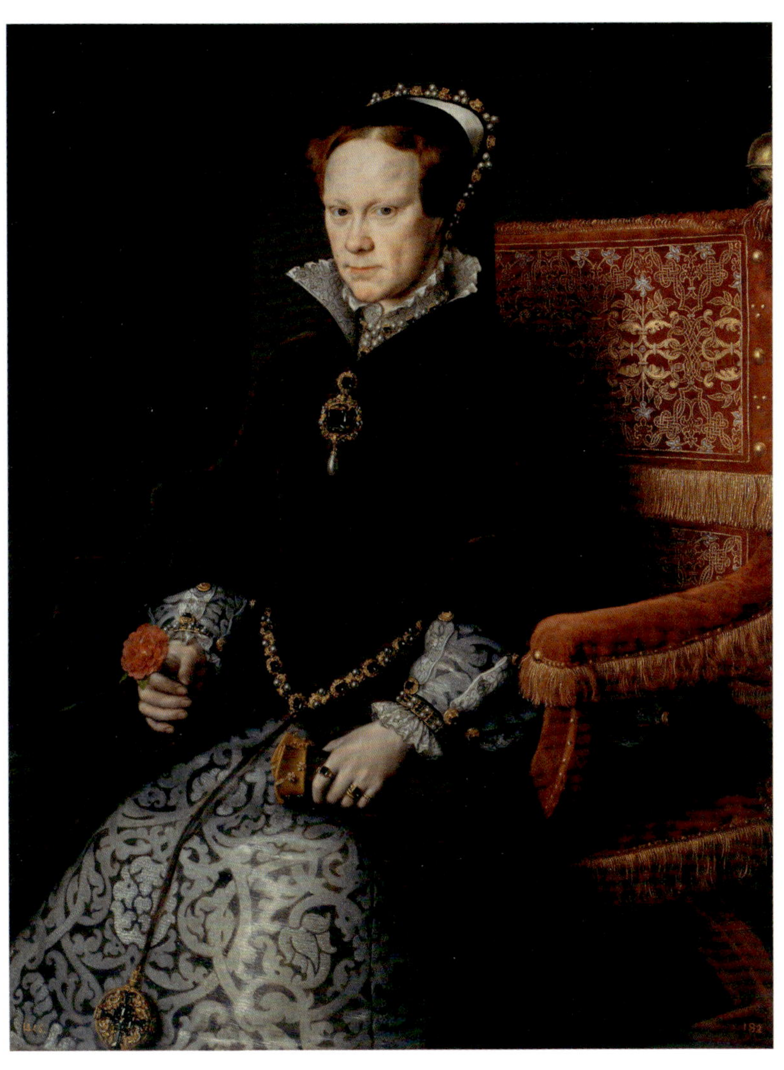

Anthonis Mor
Mary Tudor, Queen of England
1554

41

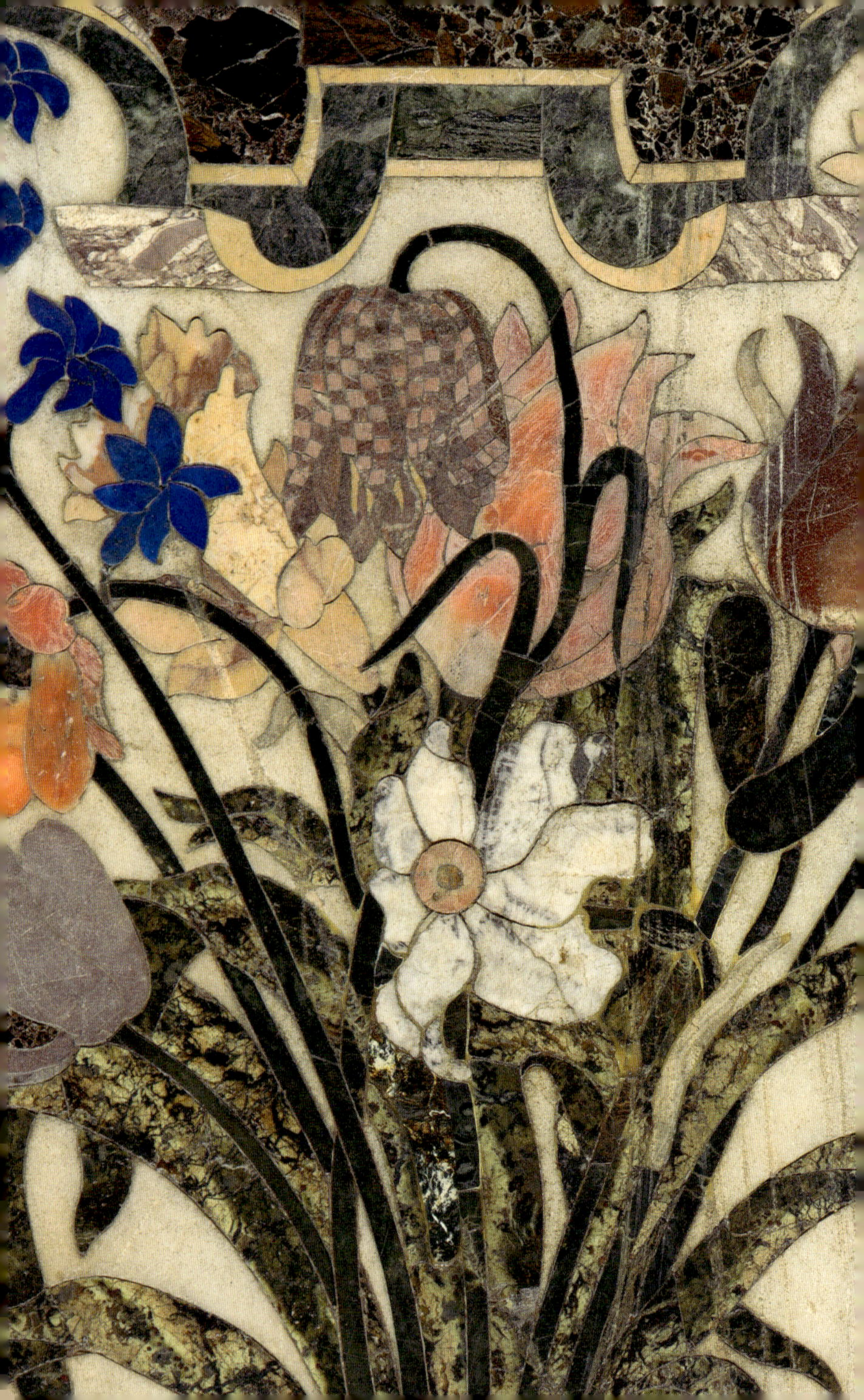

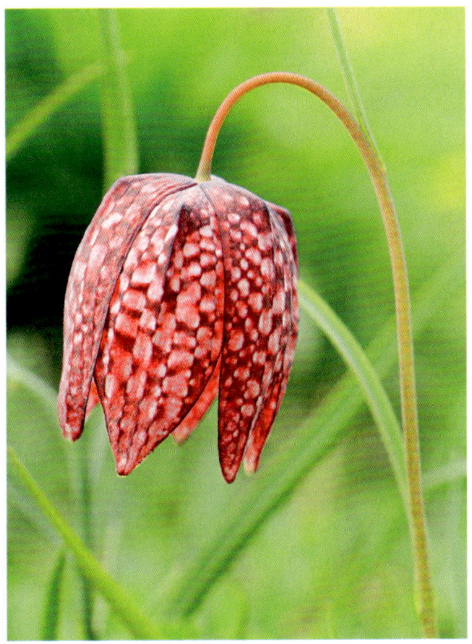

SNAKE'S HEAD

Botanical themes are addressed in art using very different materials. In this tabletop, plant species are represented in meticulously-worked semi-precious stones. A wide variety of bulb species can be seen in four carefully-arranged lapis lazuli vases. These plants have underground storage structures, from which they emerge for just a few months; afterwards, they spend the dry or cold periods buried in their bulbs or corms. One of the most surprising is the snake's head, a veritable floral fantasy.

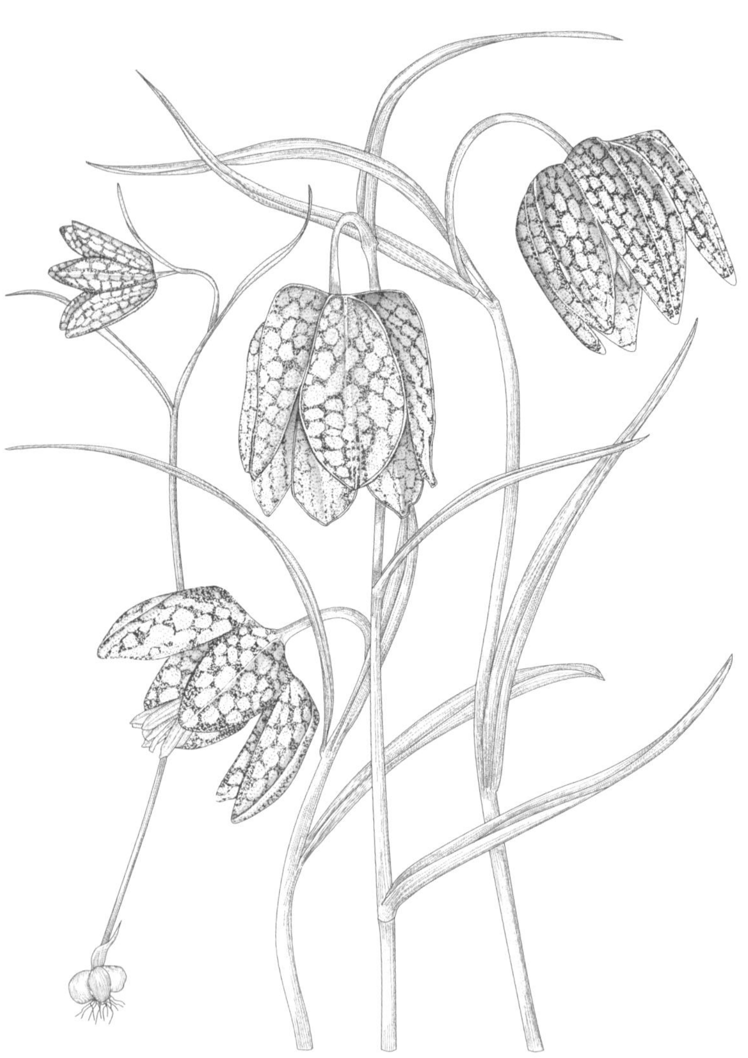

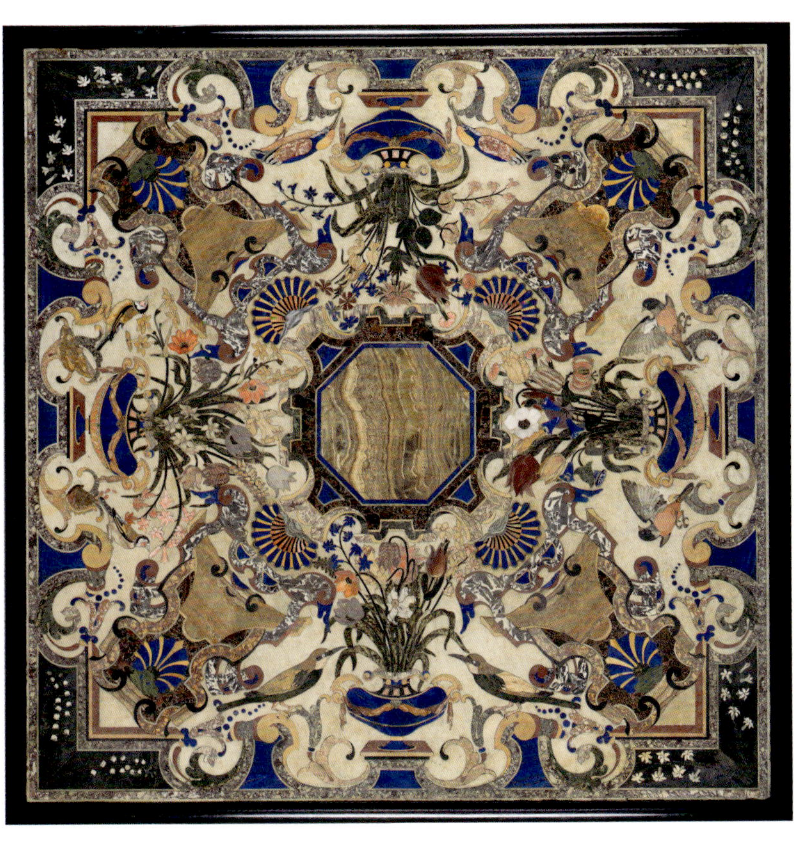

Anonymous
Tabletop of Don Rodrigo Calderón
Ca. 1615

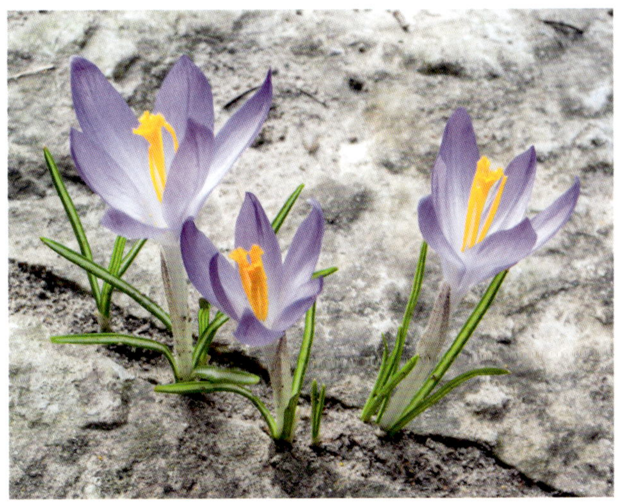

WILD SAFFRON

Nothing lasts forever, even in the plant world. Here, a withered tree has been infested by a fungus. Several carpophores – popularly known as *mushrooms* – are growing out of the trunk. Hanging from the branches is another curious organism, mid-way between the world of fungi and that of algae: a lichen called Methuselah's beard (*Dolichousnea longissima*). Below, the tip of a broken lance points to a solitary wild saffron flower; the life cycle of this bulb species symbolises the cycle of life, death and resurrection, alluded to by the crucifix visible in the upper part of the painting.

Crocus sp.

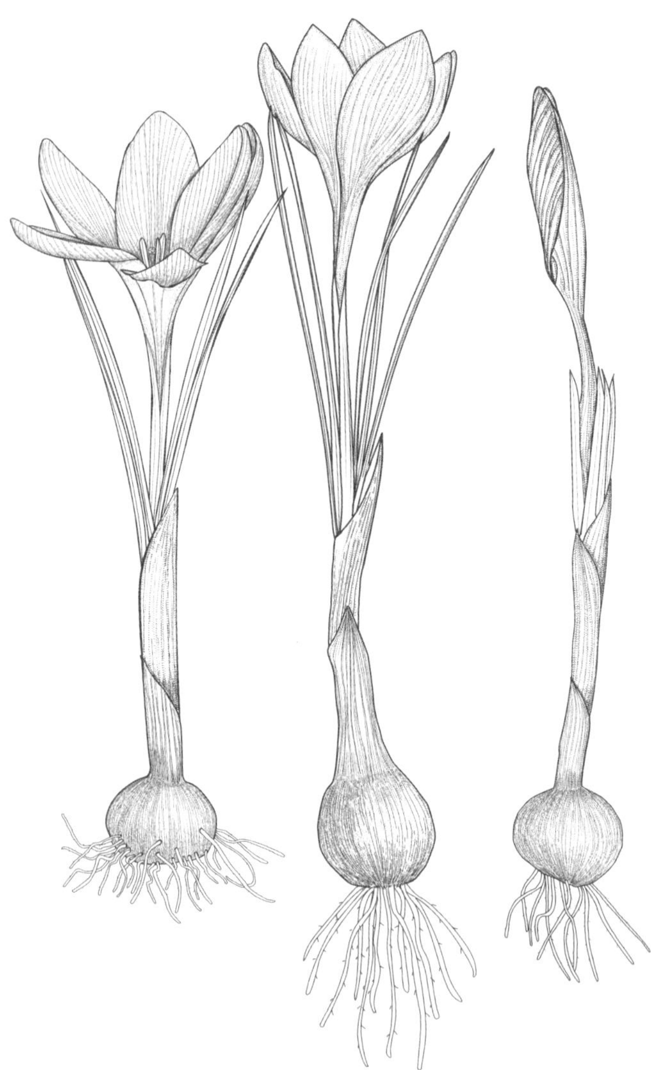

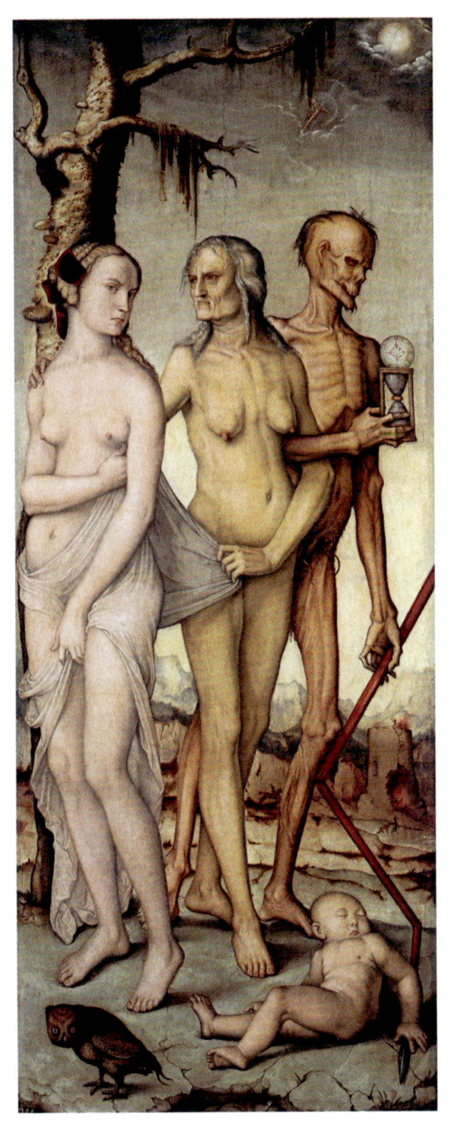

Hans Baldung Grien
The Ages of Woman and Death
1541-1544

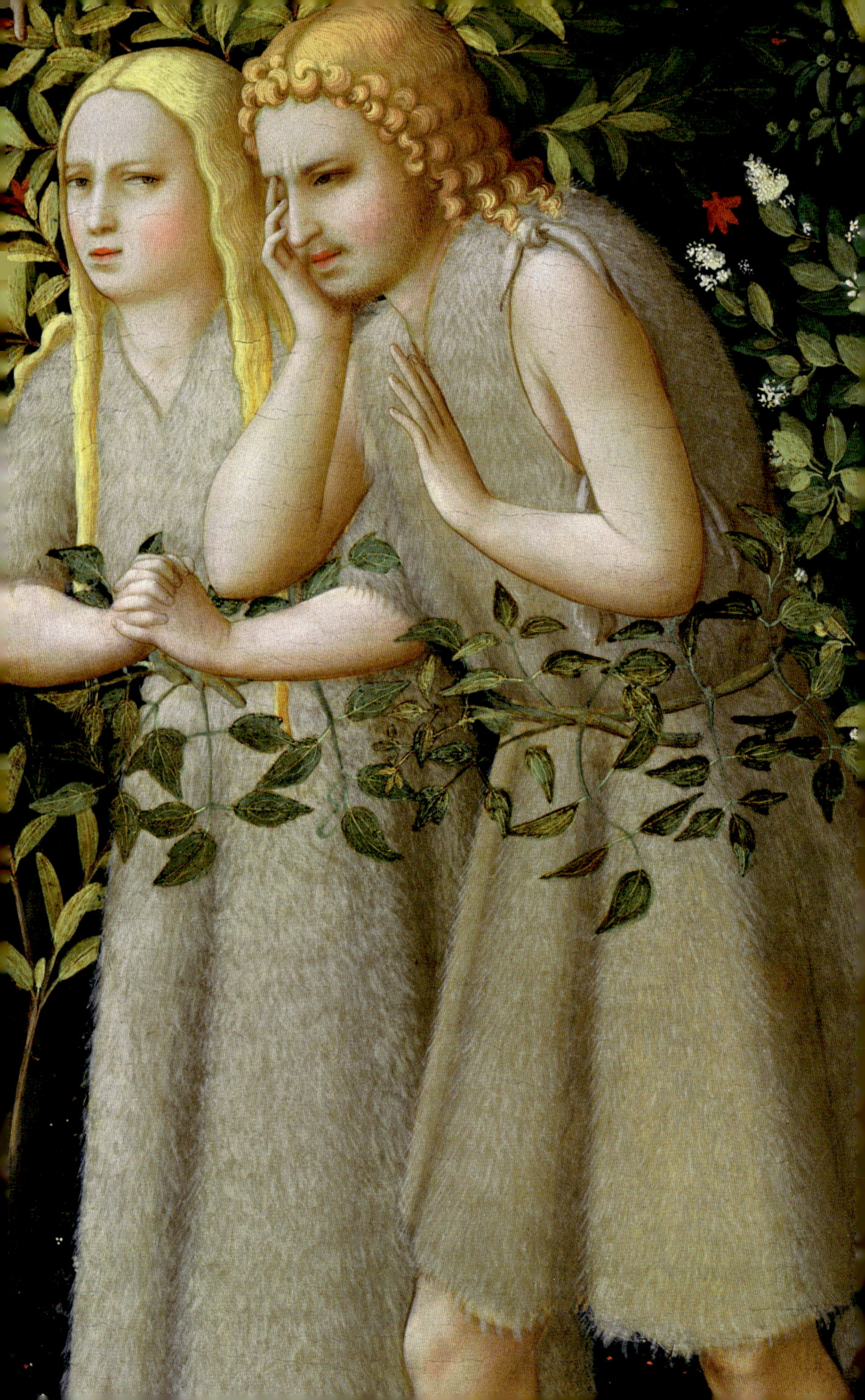

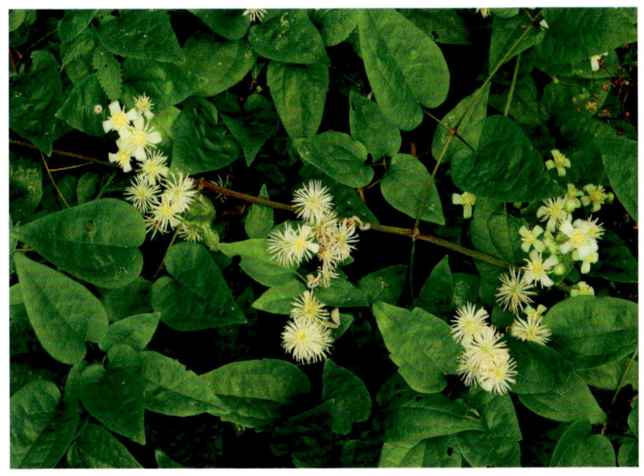

OLD MAN'S BEARD

This Garden of Eden features the four tree species re-garded as possible candidates for the Tree of the Knowl-edge of Good and Evil in the Christian tradition. The most widely-represented in that context is the apple tree (*Malus domestica*). Here, however, it is accompanied by the fig (*Ficus carica*), the bitter orange (*Citrus × aurantium*) and a pomegranate tree (*Punica granatum*) in blossom. The creeper encircling the waists of Eve and Adam is old man's beard, with which beggars would rub their skins, causing sores which might bring them more alms.

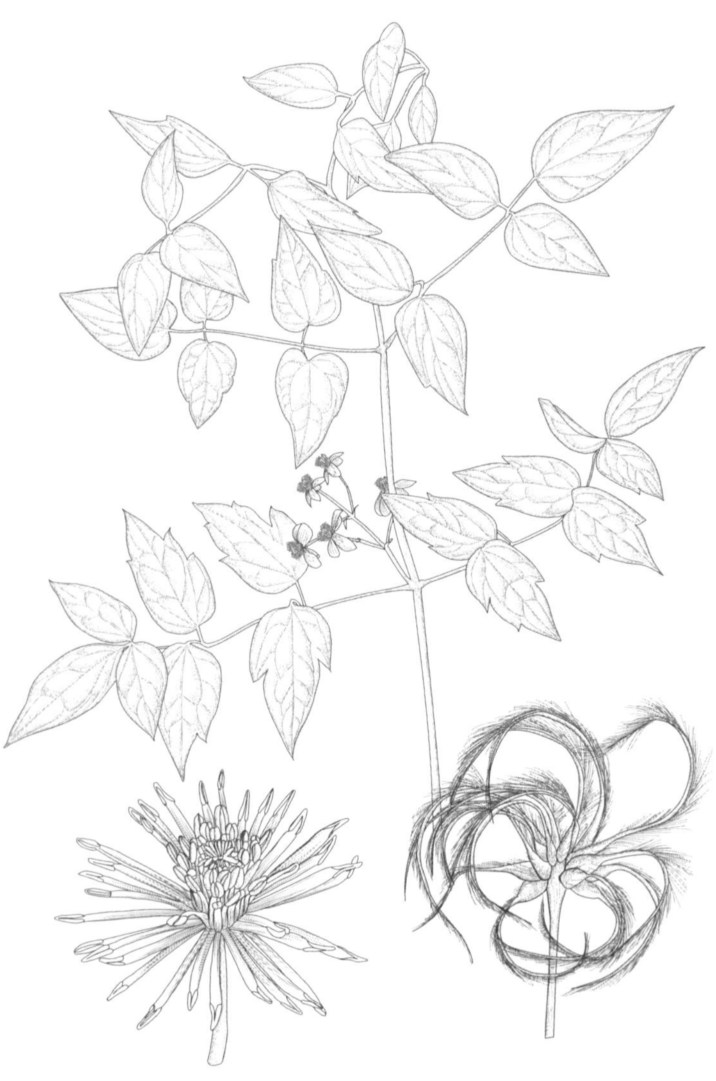

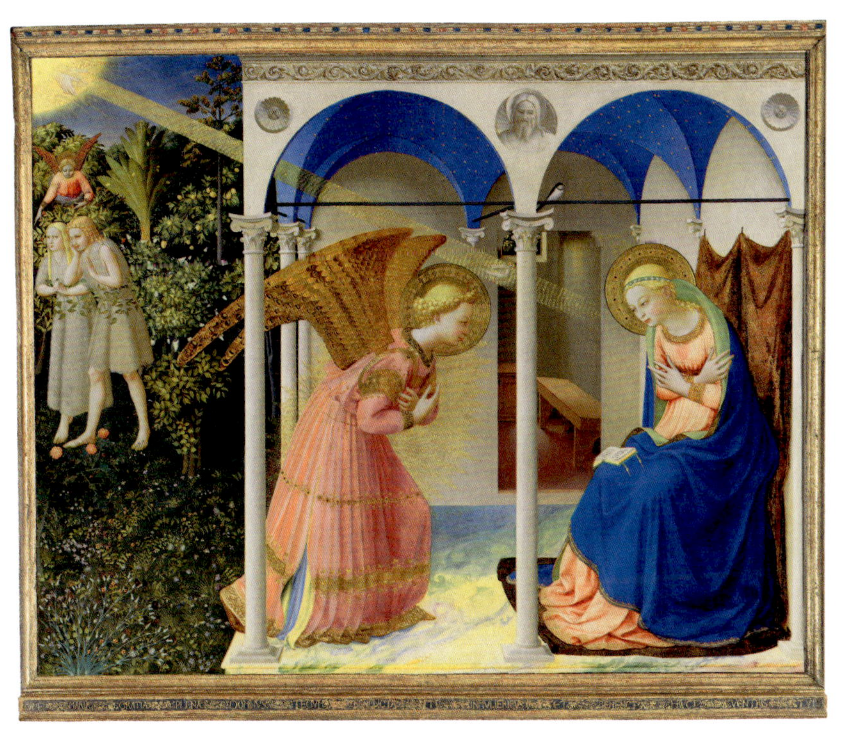

Fra Angelico
The Annunciation
Ca. 1426

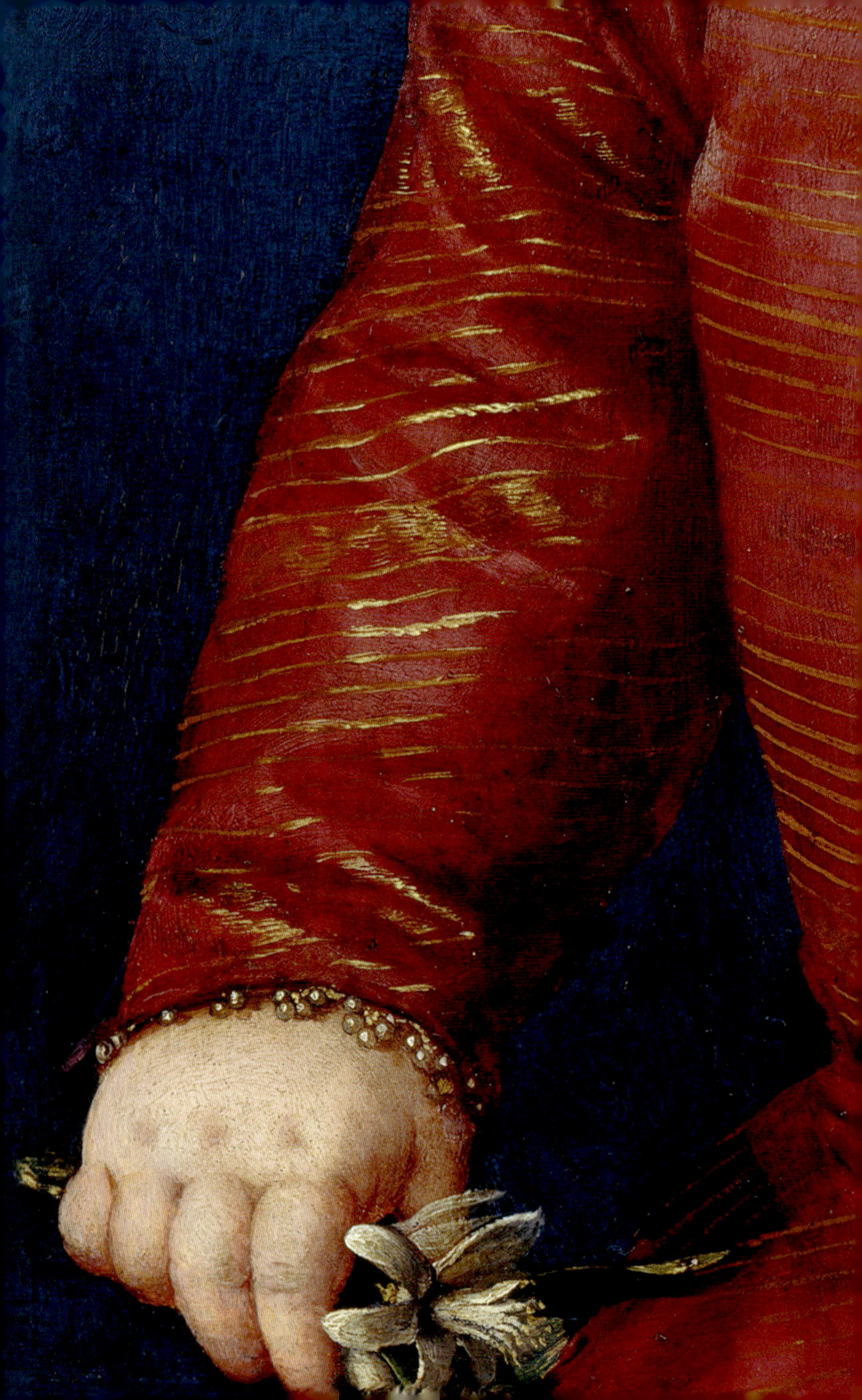

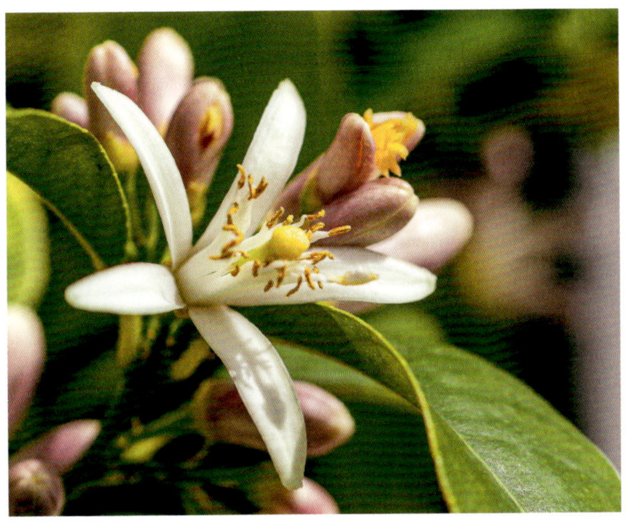

CITRON

Plant collecting is by no means a recent hobby. Citrus trees – a family that includes orange, lemon and grapefruit, among others – sparked the enthusiasm of leading families such as the Medici, in Tuscany (Italy). This dynasty created a major collection of citrus trees between the 16th and 18th centuries. The trees were grown in the open air in large terracotta pots, so that they could be transported and sheltered during the cold months in glasshouses known as *limonaie*. In this portrait, García de Medici holds a citron blossom, alluding to this family tradition.

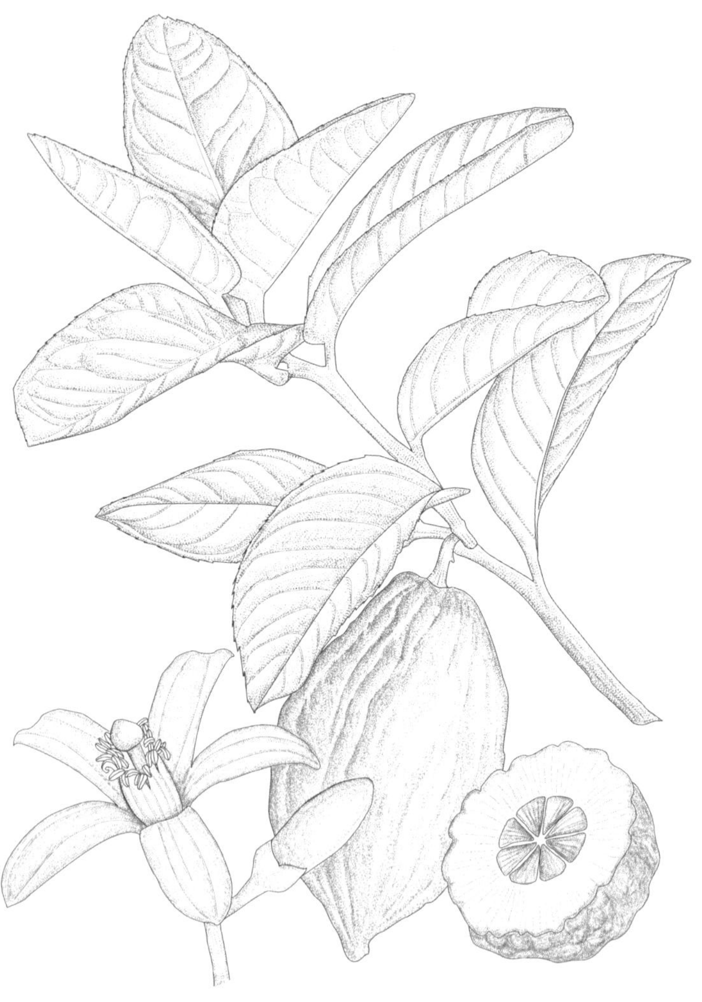

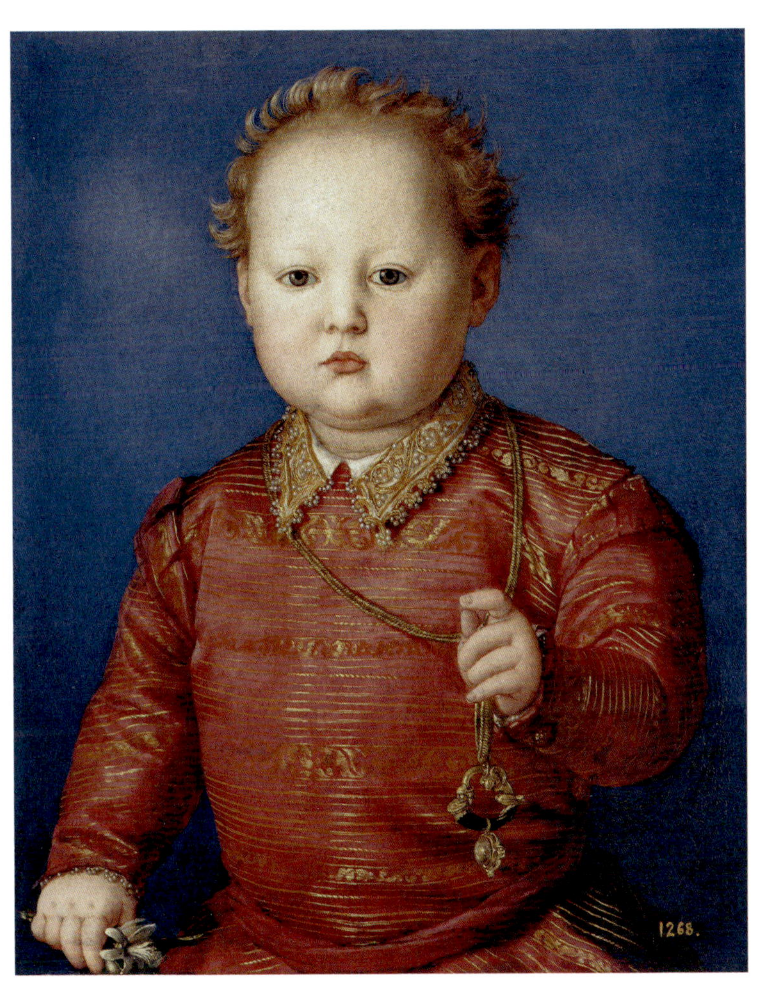

Bronzino (Agnolo di Cosimo)
García de' Medici
Ca. 1550

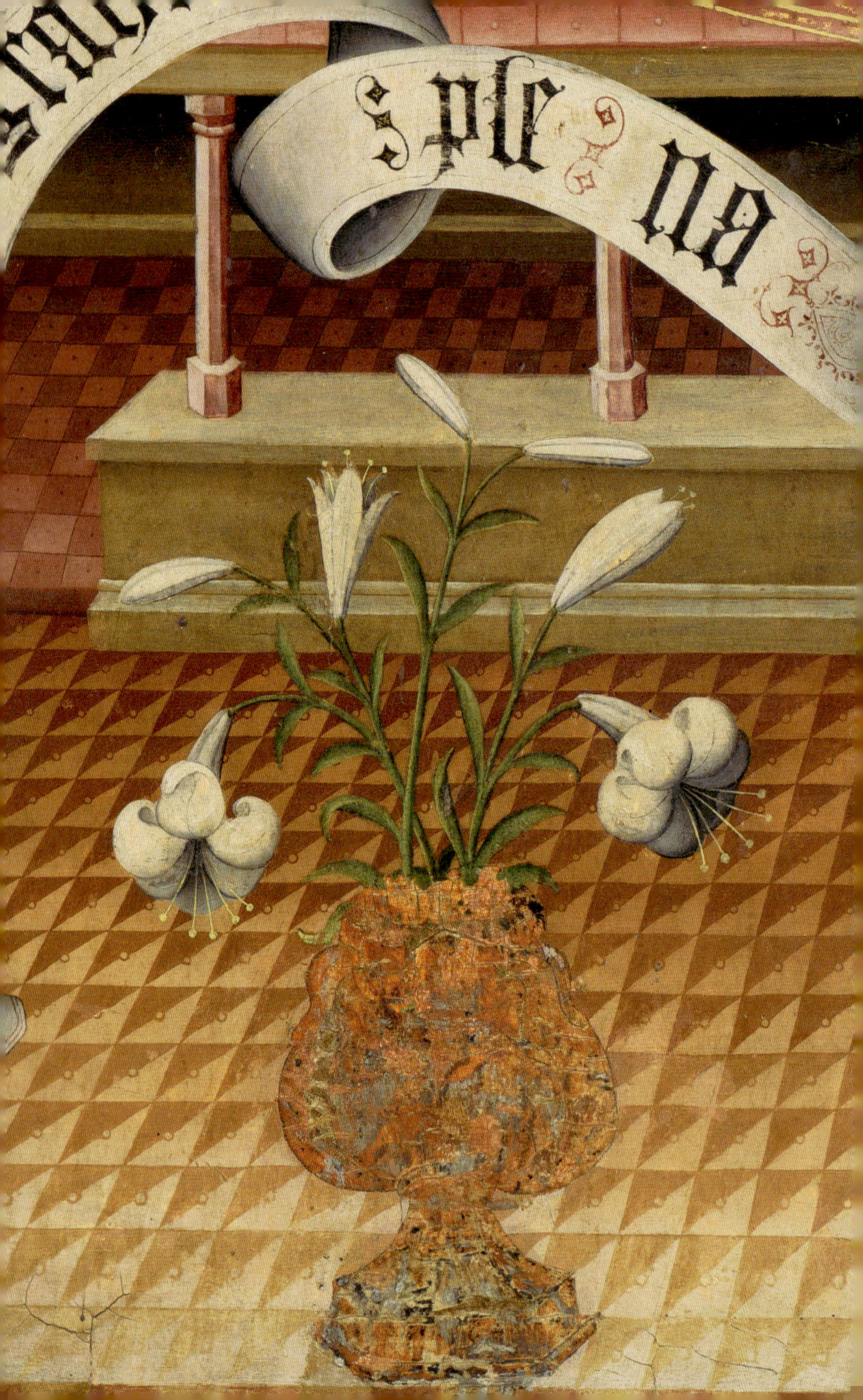
ꝯ pſe na

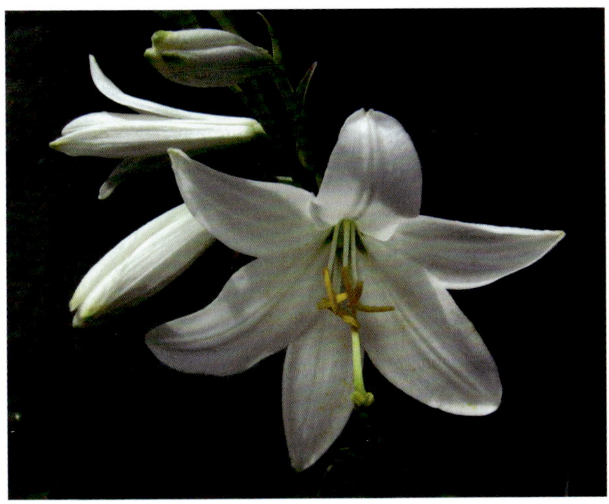

WHITE LILY

Plants – even those not producing fruit, fibres or wood – have been cultivated since time immemorial. A range of containers, such as pots or window-boxes, have long been used to bring the beauty of flowers to our very doorsteps. In this scene, which is more traditional than religious, an angel uses a pulley to draw a bucket of water from the well, in order to water the plants (detail page 4). Nearby is a vase full of white lilies, one of the five flowers most frequently depicted in the Museo del Prado, symbolising Mary's purity and virginity.

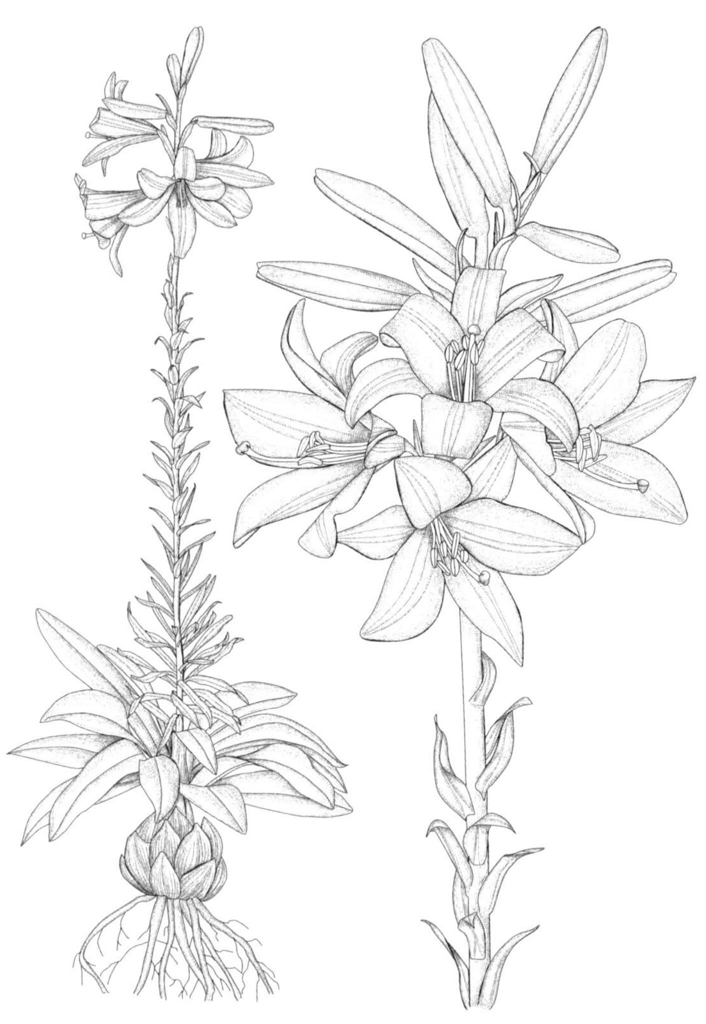

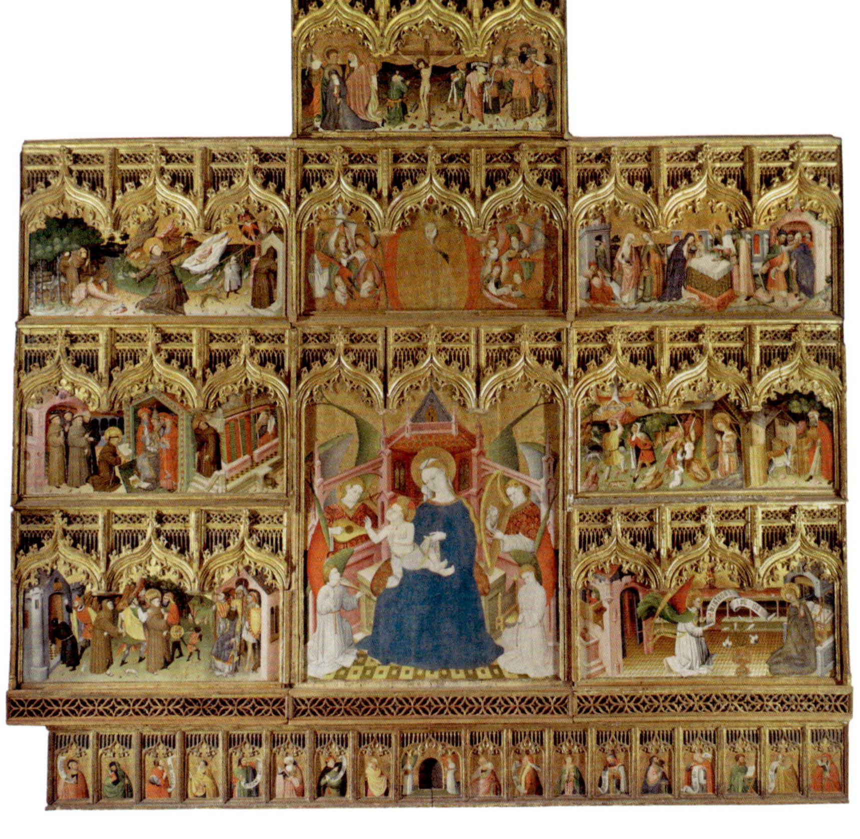

Nicolás Francés
Altarpiece of the Lives of the Virgin and Saint Francis
1445-1460

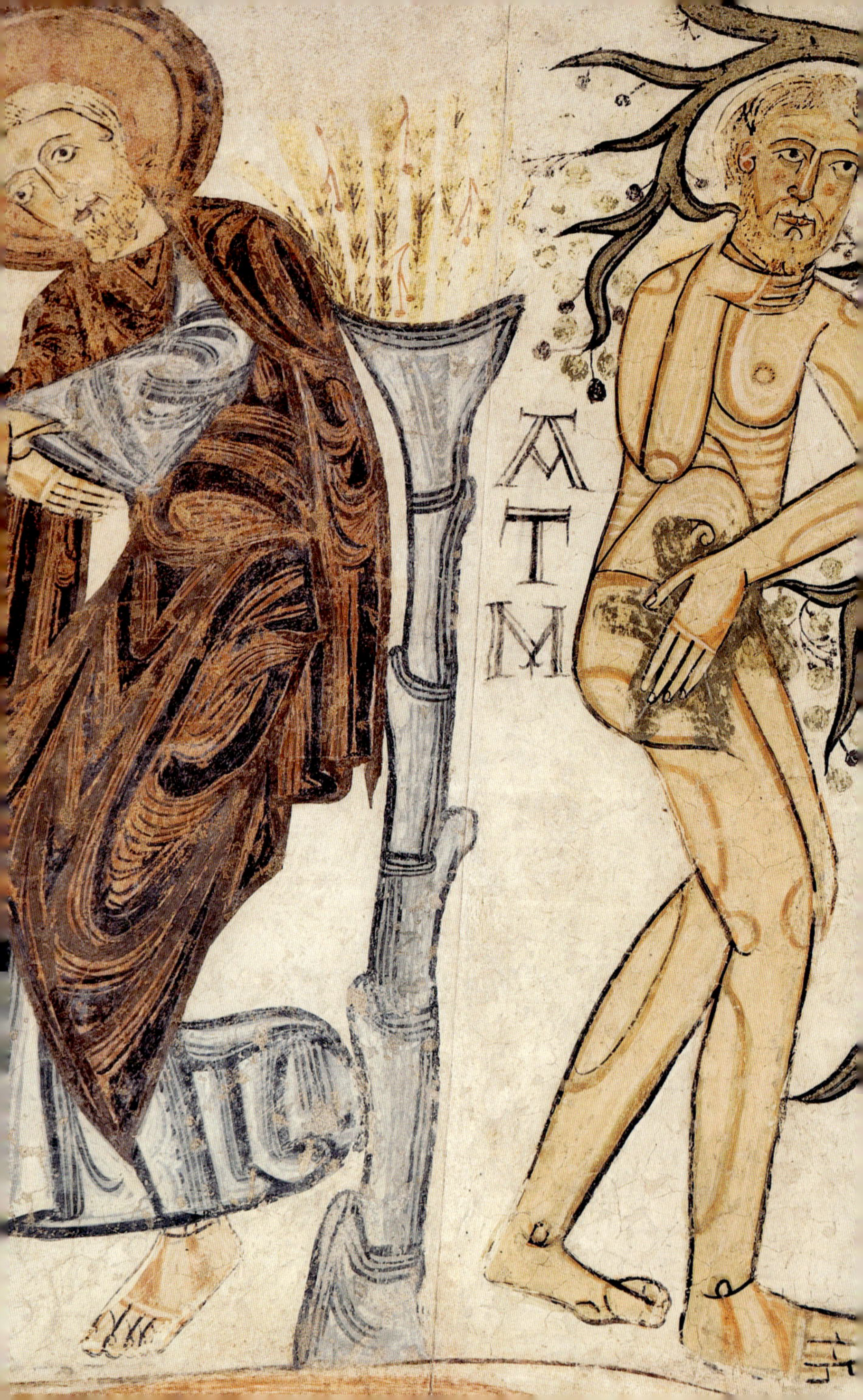

A
T
M

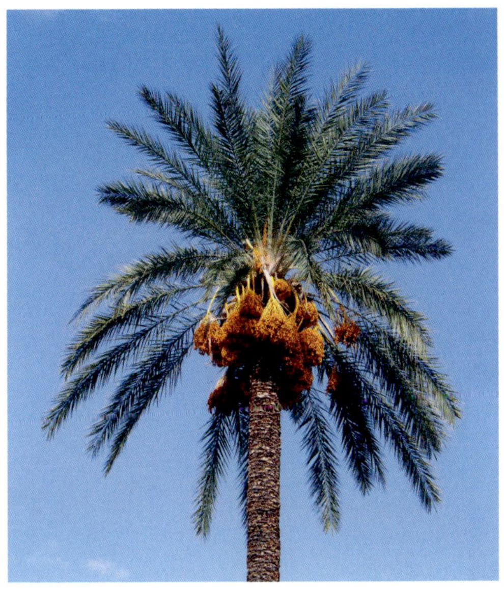

DATE PALM

A date palm serves to separate these two scenes from Genesis. This species is a constant in the history of art, having been used since classical antiquity to enhance the surroundings of sanctuaries. The palm tree, a symbol of paradise, is commonly found in depictions of the Garden of Eden, like this one. Here, the tree is represented schematically, with compound leaves and red bunches of dates emerging from an unreal articulated trunk or stipe. On the right, Adam and Eve cover their nakedness with fig leaves (*Ficus carica*).

Phoenix dactylifera

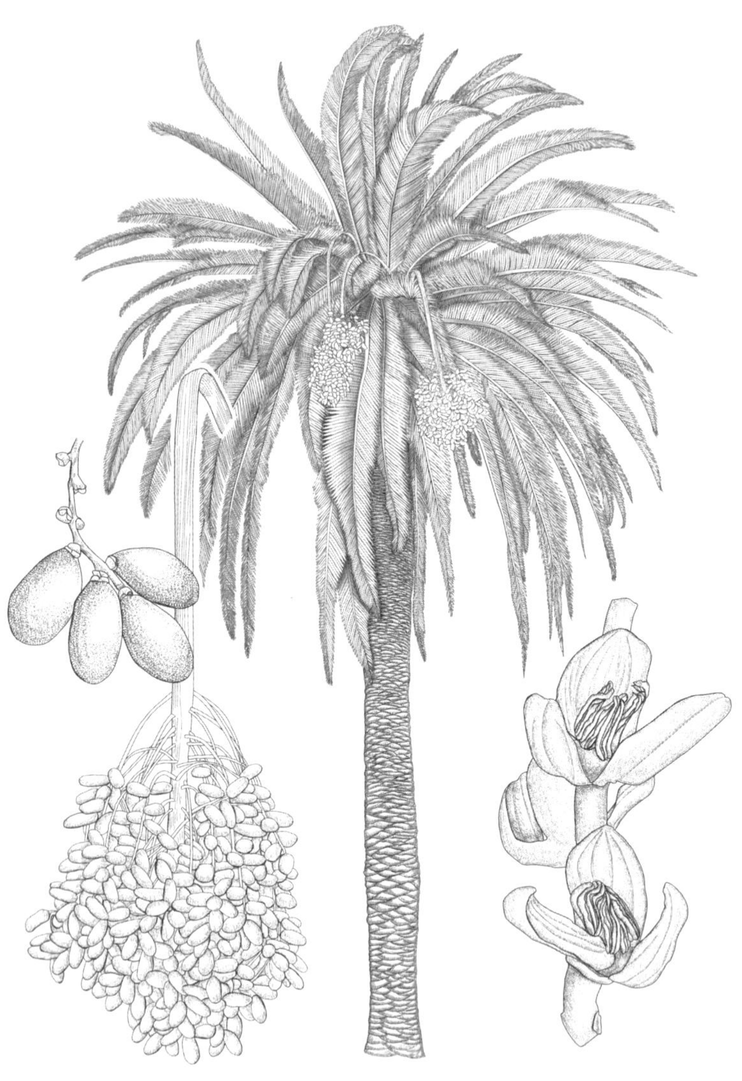

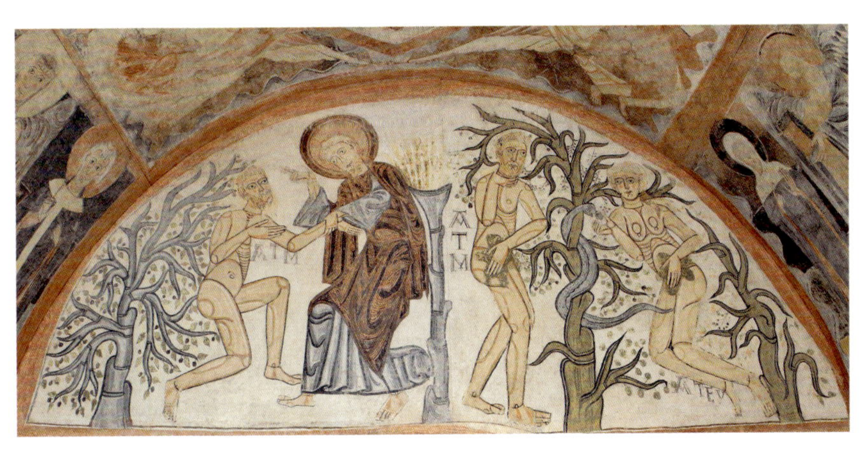

Anonymous
The Creation of Adam and *Original Sin*
Hermitage of Vera Cruz, Maderuelo (Segovia)
12th century

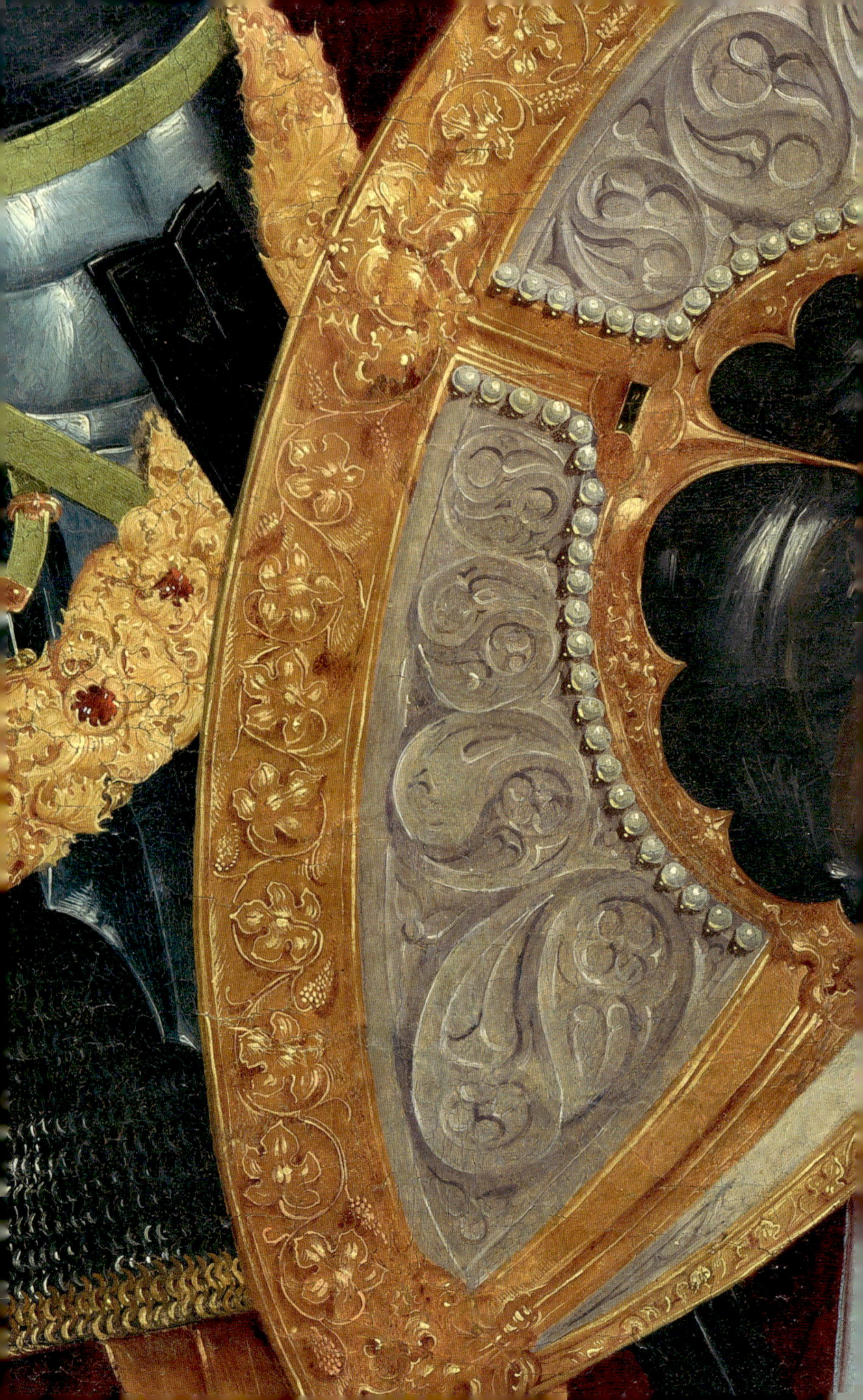

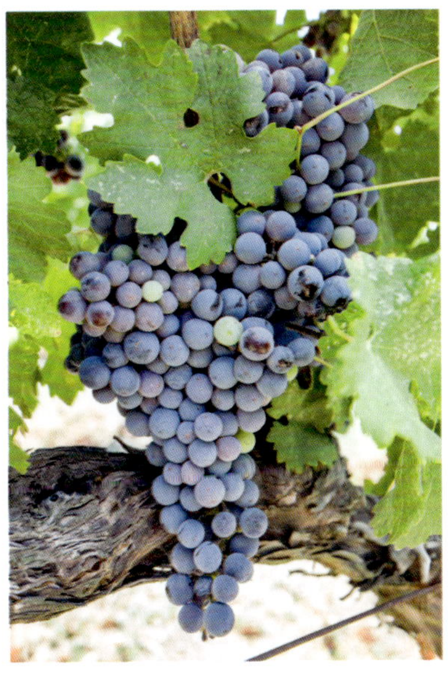

COMMON GRAPEVINE

Botany is not always apparent in works of art. It is often hidden. No one would say that there were any plants in this painting, and yet there are a few waiting to be discovered. The archangel's golden girdle is made of intertwined thistle leaves (*Cirsium* sp.), a symbol of Christ's Passion. Similarly, the shield with which he protects himself has an ornamental border of grapevine leaves and bunches of grapes, an allusion to the blood shed by Christ in his martyrdom.

Vitis vinifera

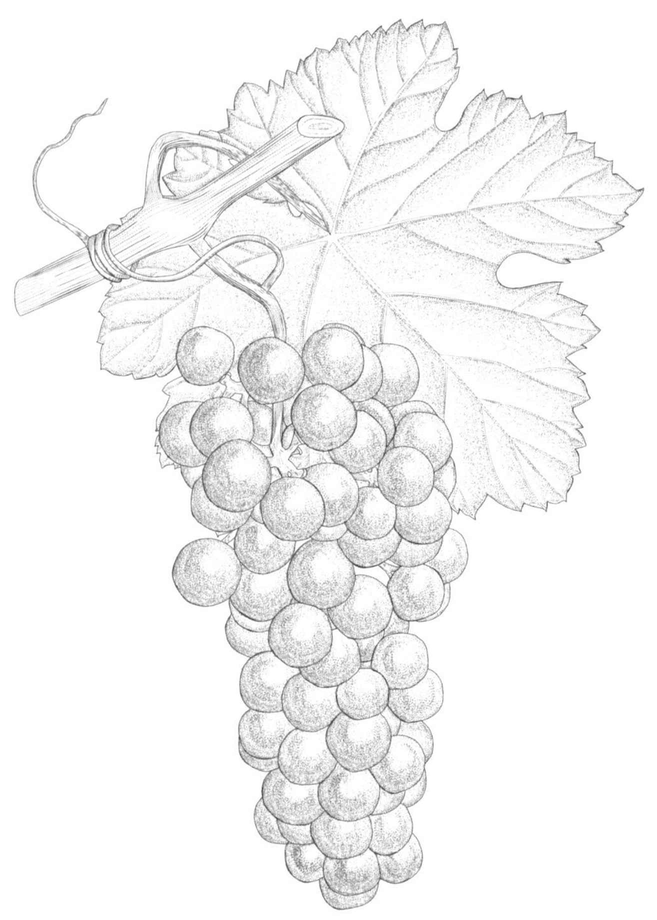

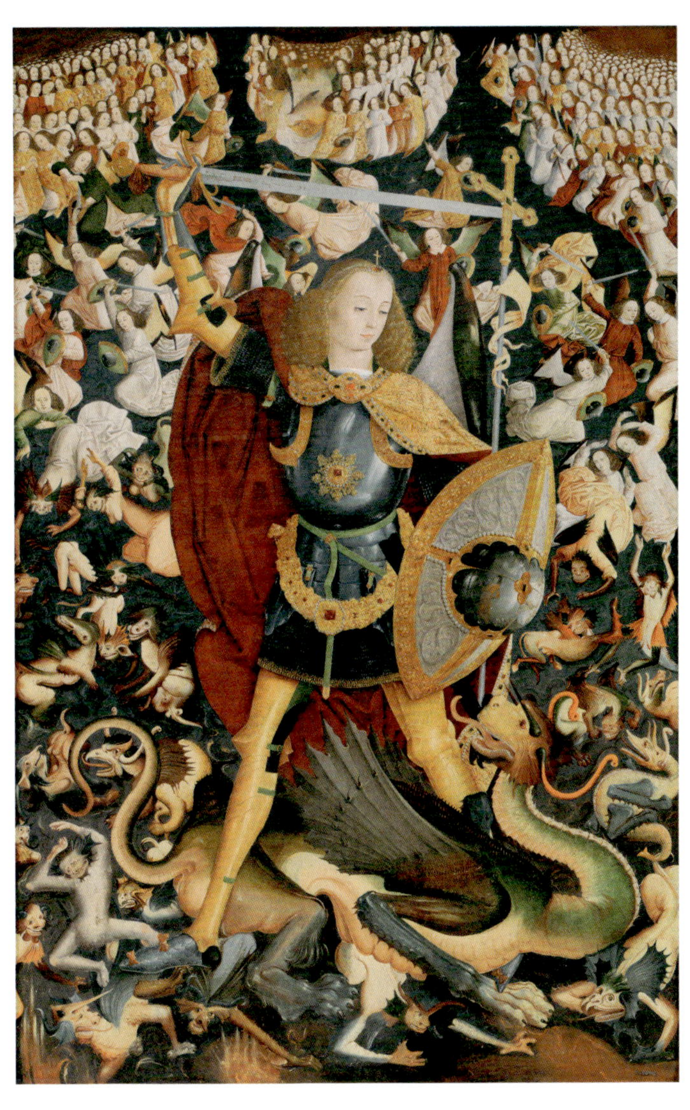

Master of Zafra
Saint Michael the Archangel
1495-1500

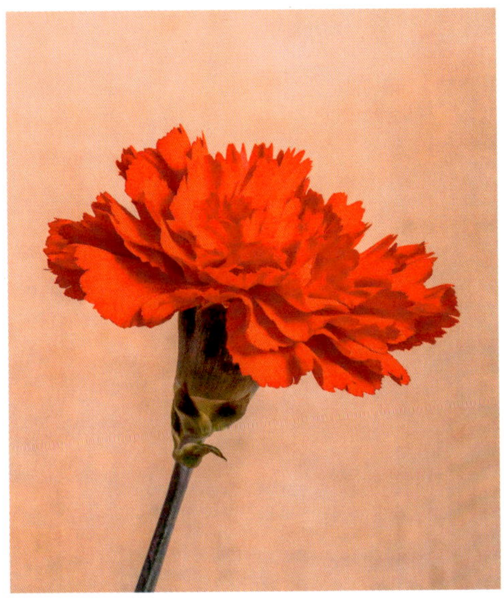

CARNATION

The central female figure is holding a carnation, here intended to symbolise betrothal or emotional commitment. In many wedding portraits, particularly in northern Europe, the bride and groom are shown holding carnations. To the right of the woman's face is a white rose of York (*Rosa × alba* 'Semi-plena'), with numerous white petals and yellow stamens. This variety has a sweet, intense scent, as do the white and pink common stock (*Matthiola incana*), depicted here with their four characteristic petals, for example in several of the bouquets adorning the drapery.

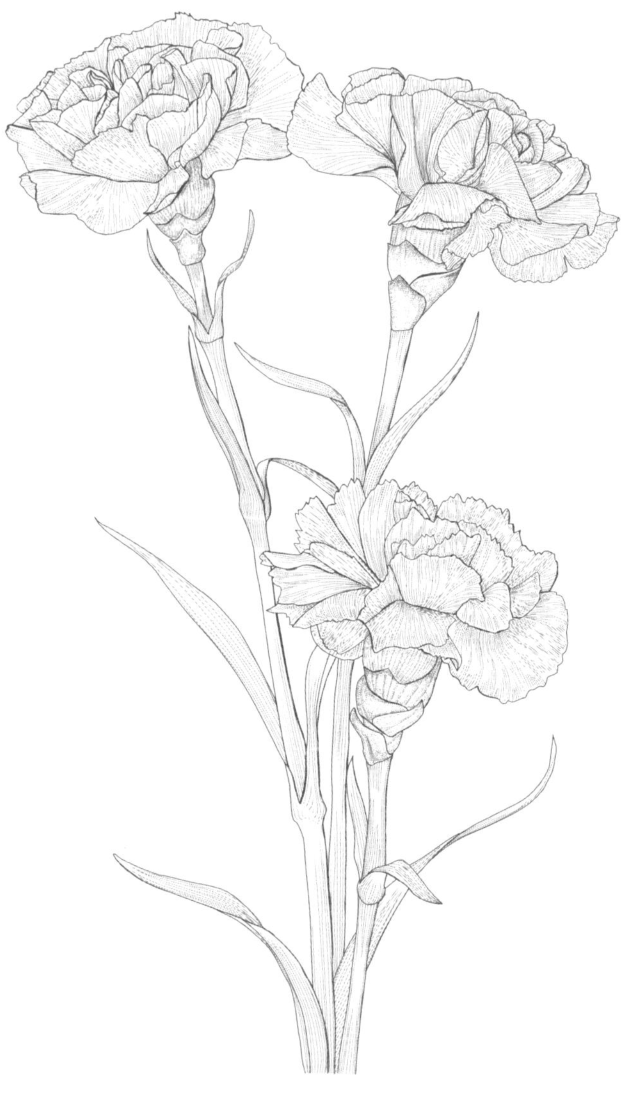

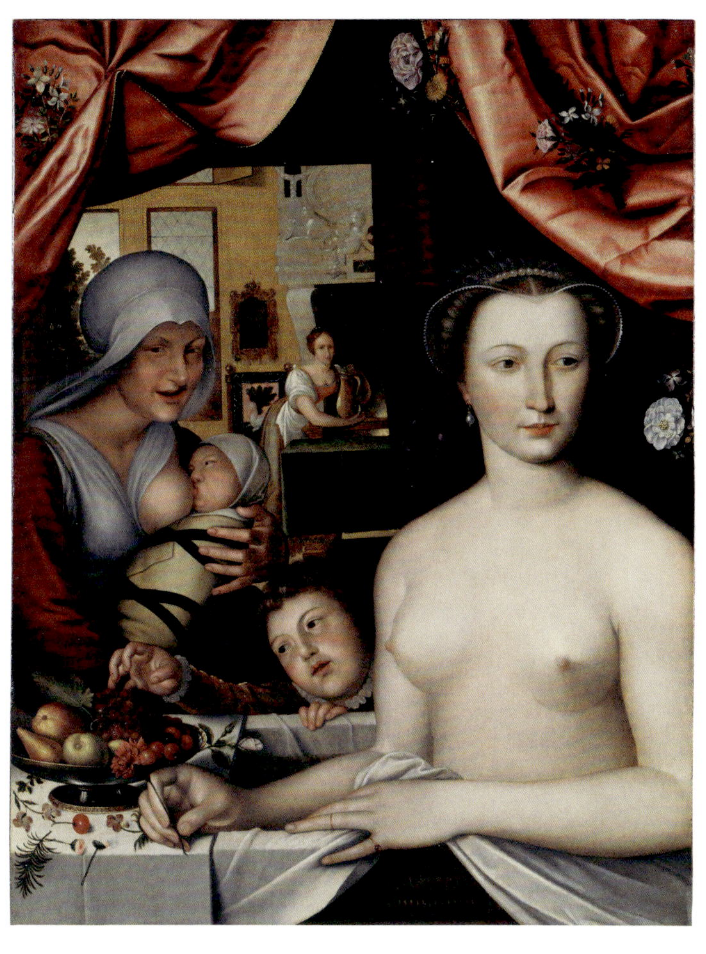

Workshop of François Clouet
A Lady in her Bath (Diane de Poitiers?)
Ca. 1566

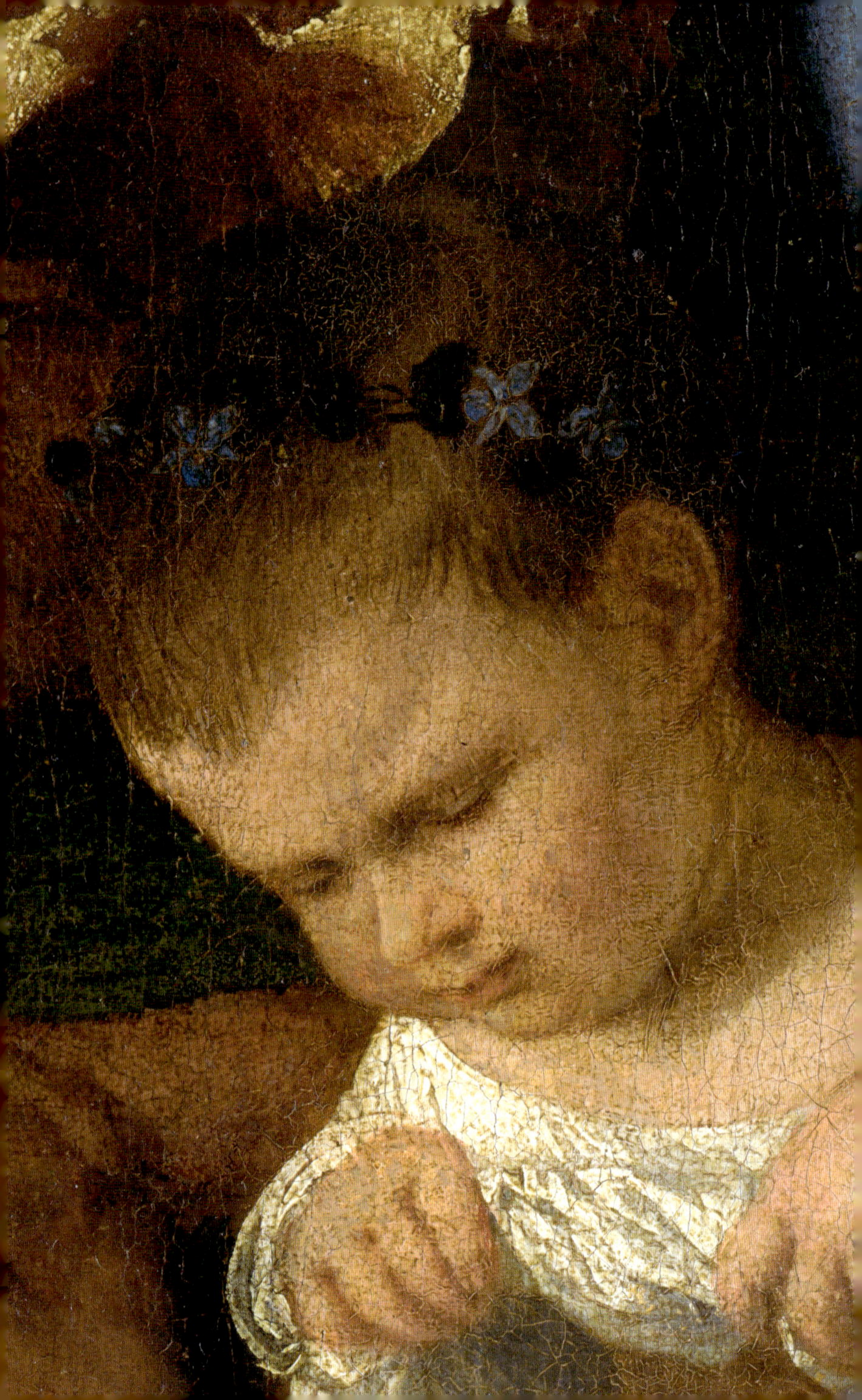

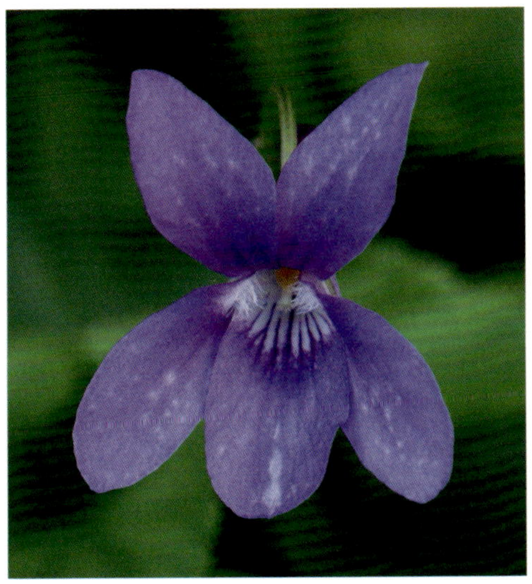

SWEET VIOLET

The sweet violet, whose edible flower has a fascinating scent, is a small, modest plant. Even so, it has been widely depicted in art for centuries. This may be due in part to its association with Aphrodite, the Greek goddess of love. In the bacchanal shown here, one of the women wears violets over her ear and in her cleavage, perhaps intended as a nod to Violante, the artist's partner. The child is also crowned with a garland of violet leaves and flowers, regarded by the ancient Greeks as a remedy for hangovers.

Viola odorata

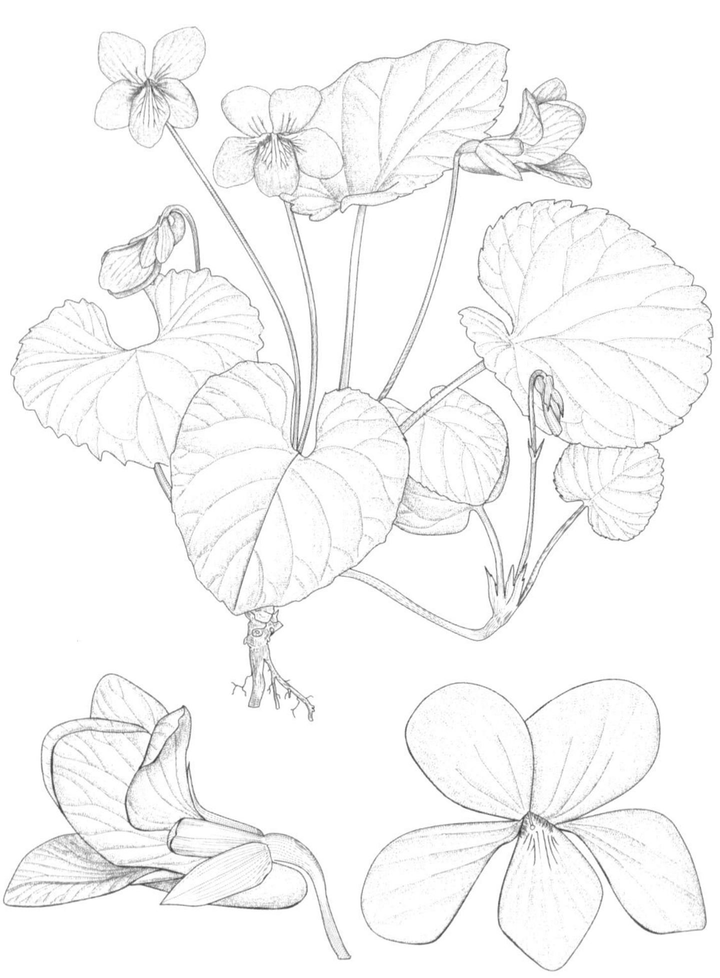

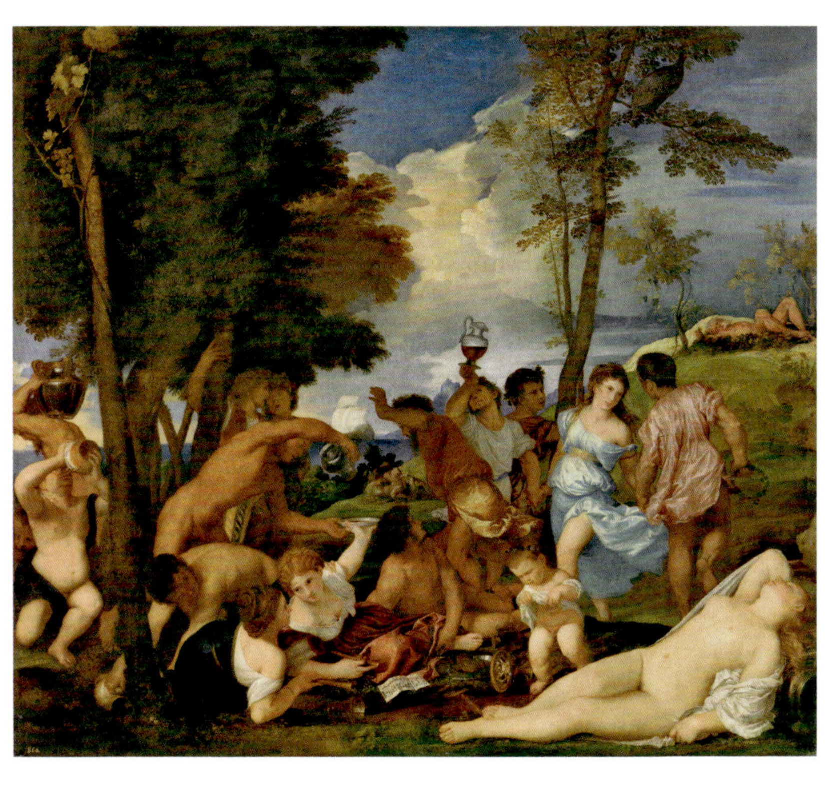

Titian (Tiziano Vecellio)
The Andrians
1523-1526

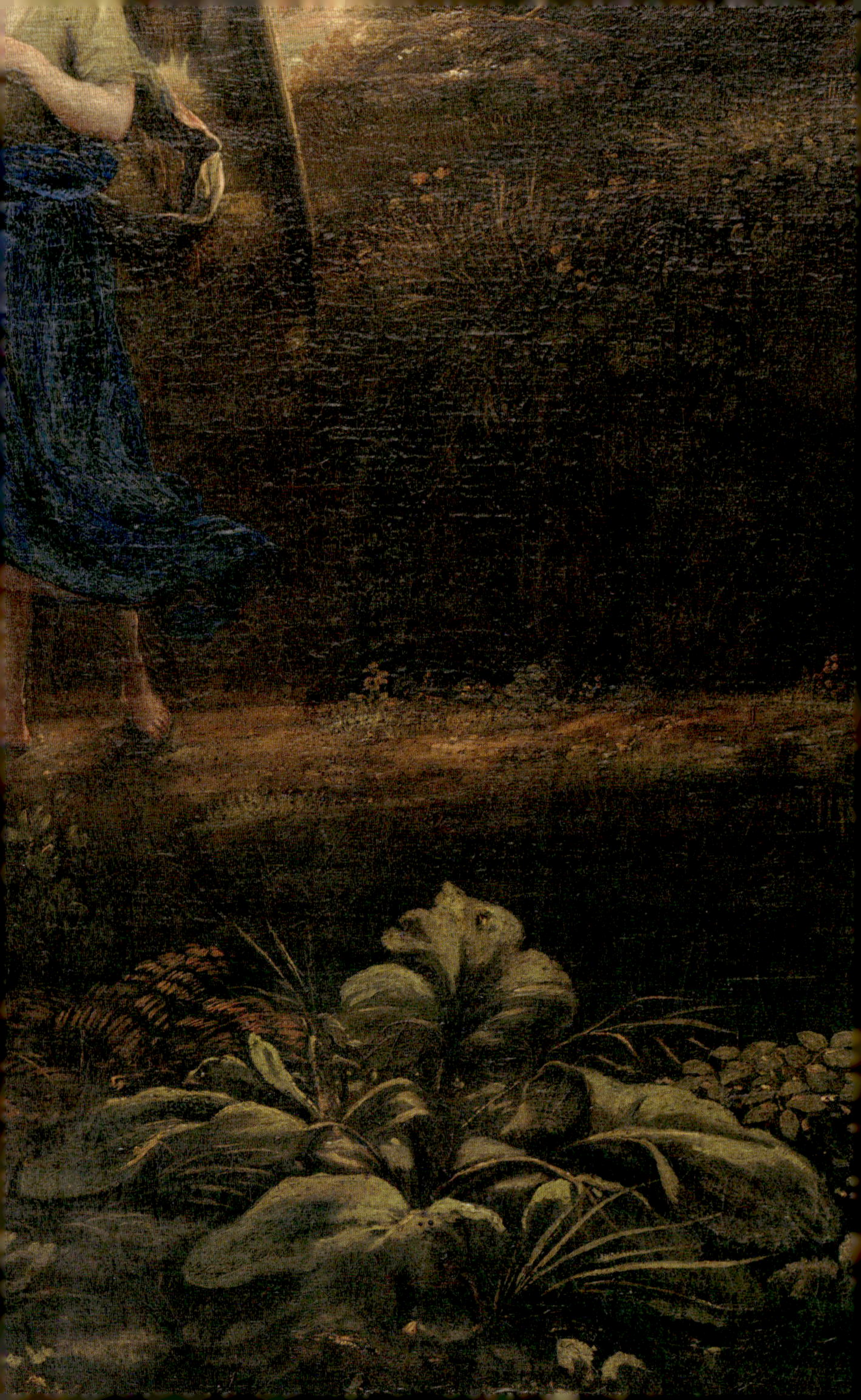

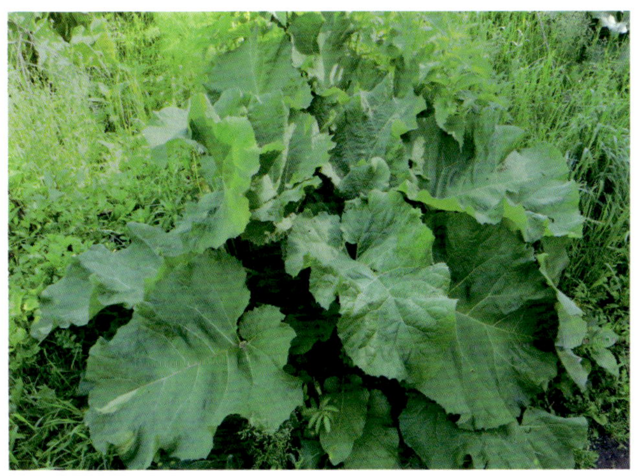

GREATER BURDOCK

An enormous stone pine (*Pinus pinea*), identifiable by its large umbrella-shaped crown, rises up on the right of this painting. It helps to make the landscape seem larger and the figures smaller. It is among the plants that must have appealed to Claude Lorrain in Rome, where he spent much of his life, and it still provides one of the city's most recognisable botanical silhouettes. In the foreground, Lorrain has included another very singular plant: the greater burdock, a species whose huge herbaceous leaves are particularly striking.

Arctium cf. *lappa*

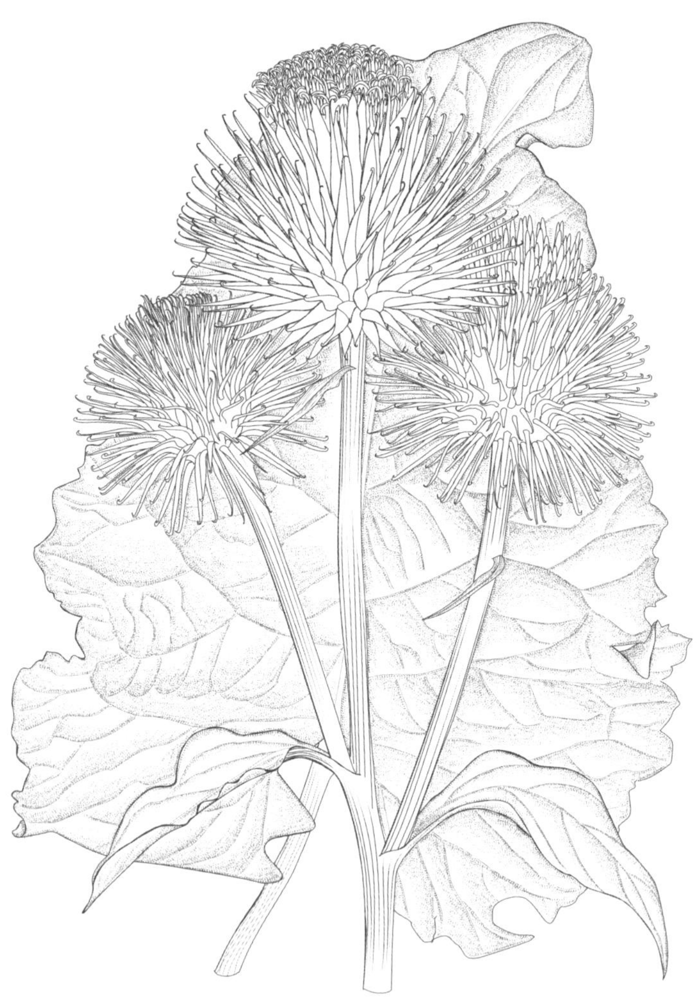

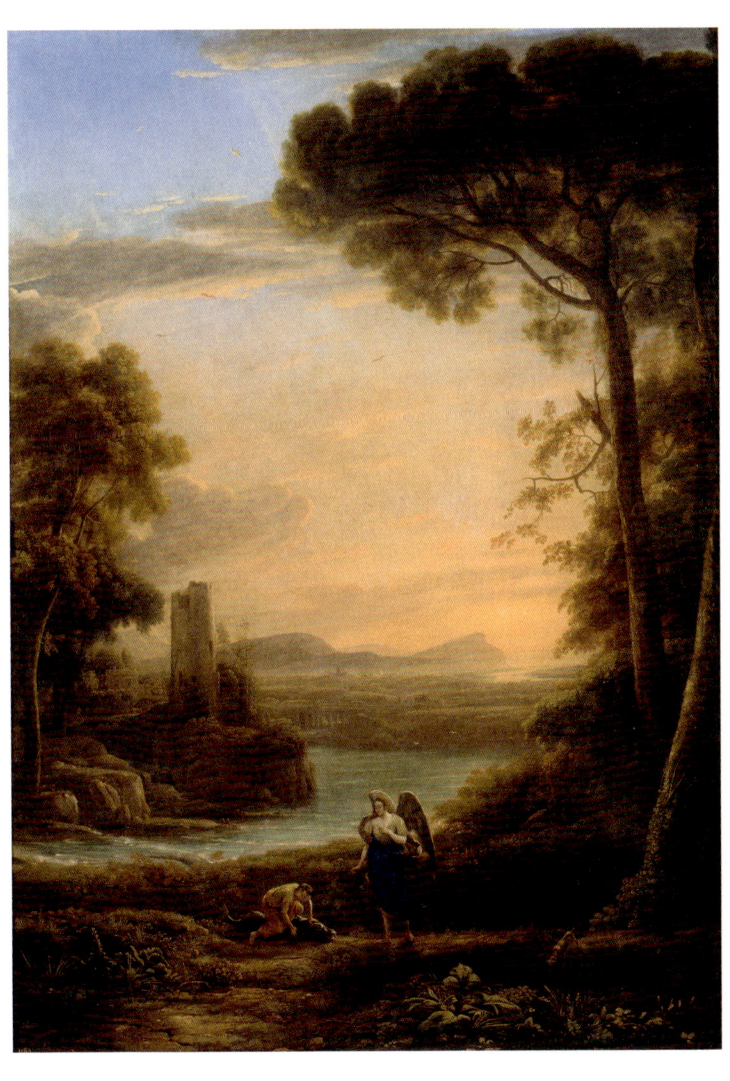

Claude Lorrain (byname of Claude Gellée Lorrain)
The Archangel Raphael and Tobias
1639-1640

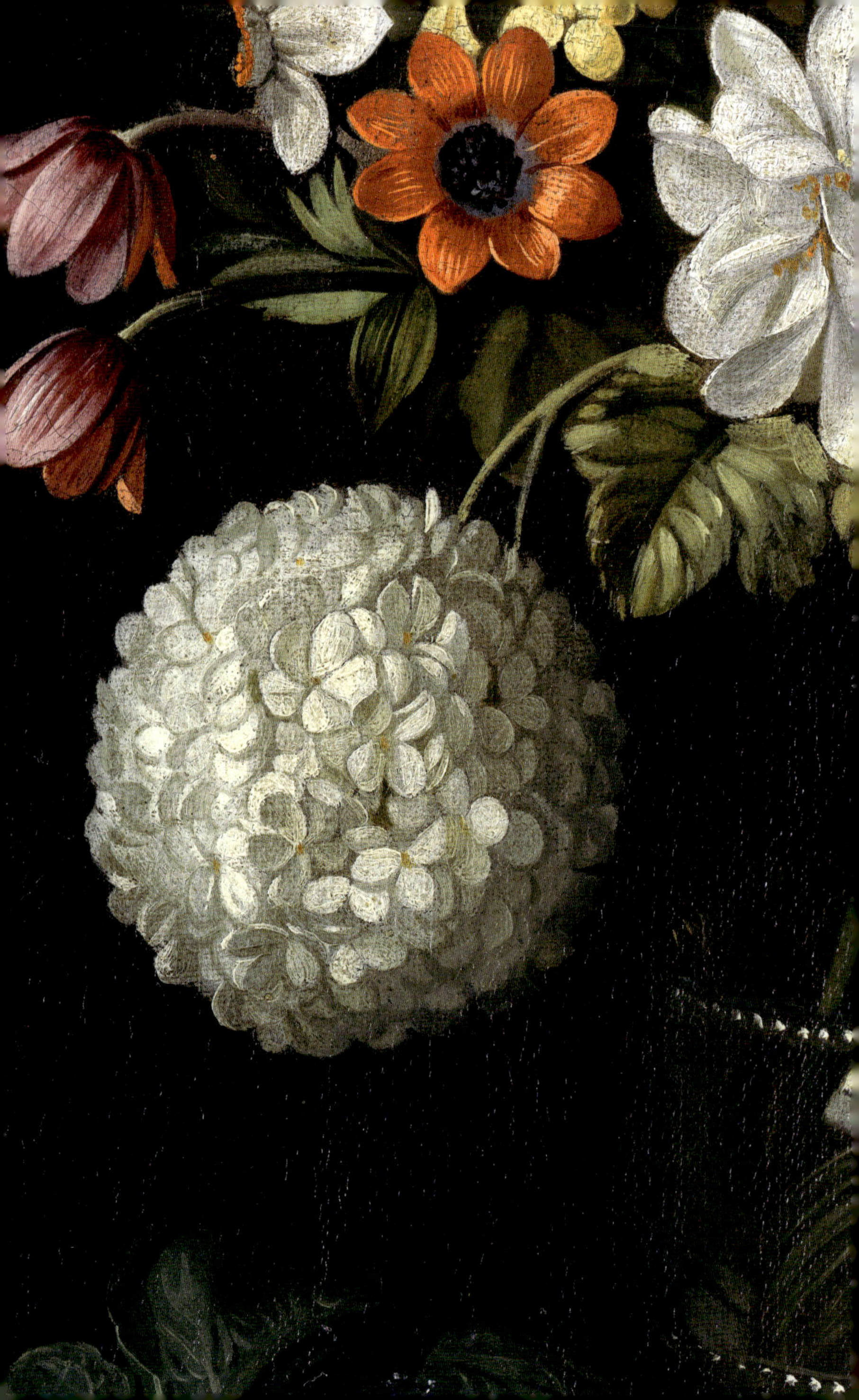

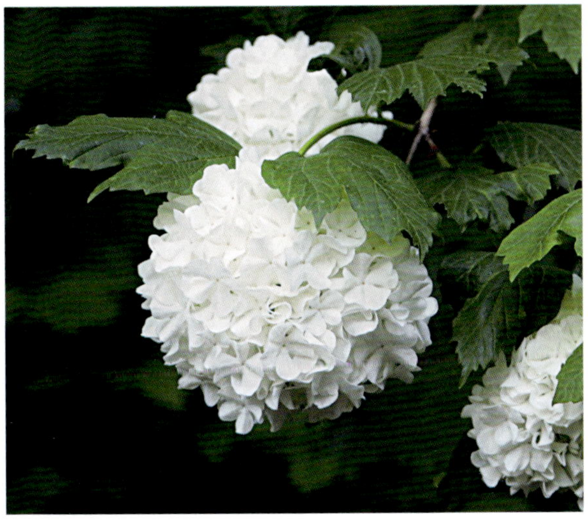

GUELDER ROSE

In the large central vase, the artist has created a floral symphony remarkable for the interplay of colours. Within the composition, each flower is matched by a counterpart identical or similar in colour: there are two blue bearded irises (*Iris × germanica*), two red and two yellow tulips (*Tulipa* cv.), two mauve anemones (*Anemone hortensis*) at the centre of the bouquet, and so on... Below them, our attention is drawn by the almost perfectly-spherical inflorescences of two guelder roses, a plant much appreciated by Baroque painters and also by present-day gardeners.

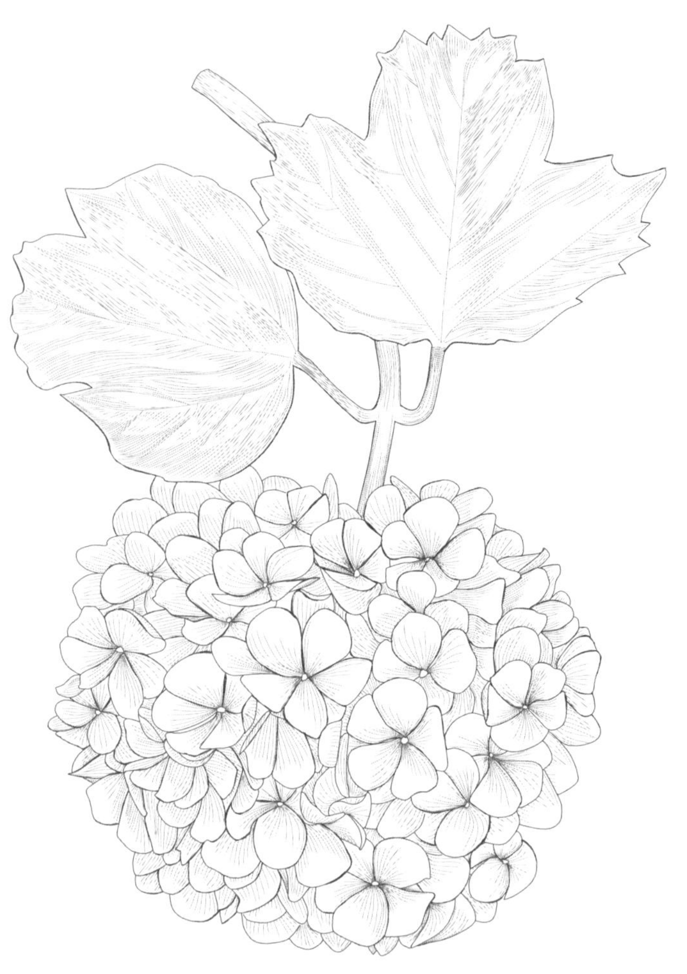

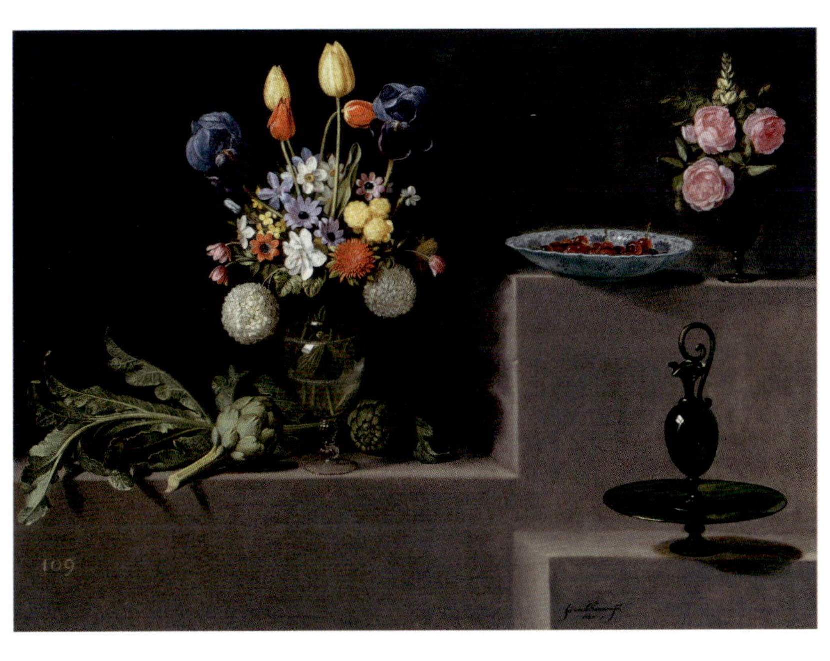

Juan van der Hamen y León
Still Life with Artichokes, Flowers and Glass Vessels
1627

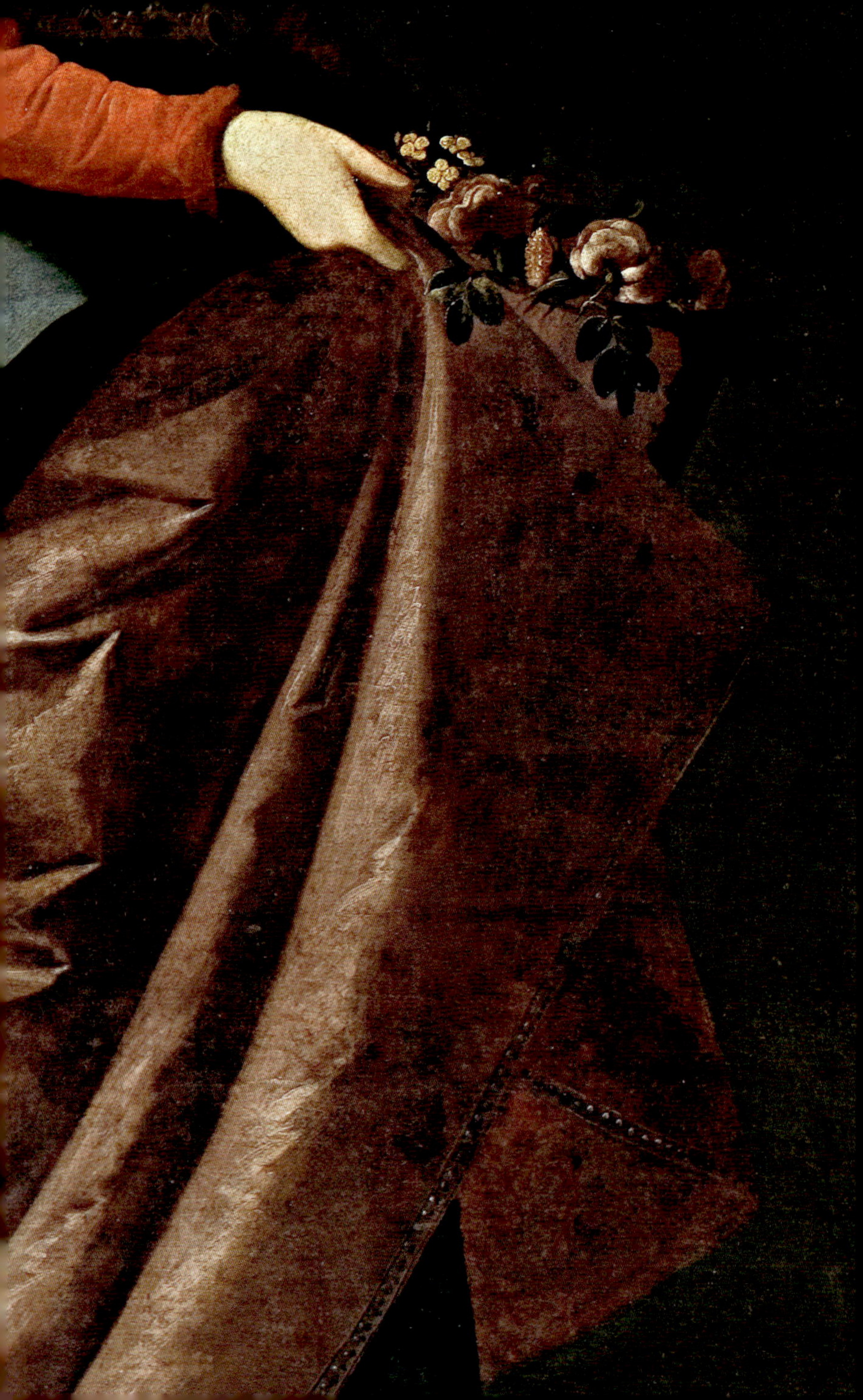

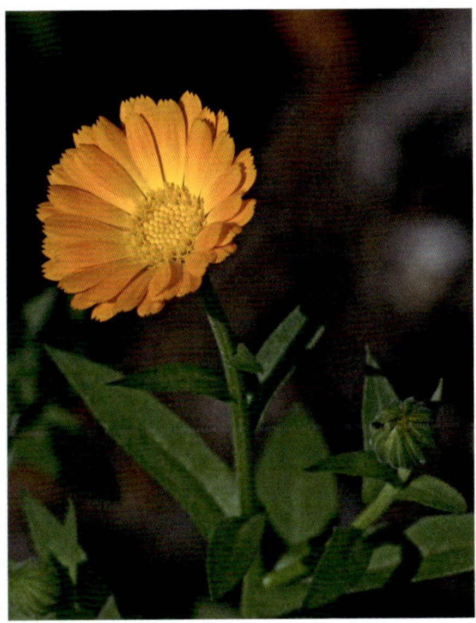

COMMON MARIGOLD

The coins carried in the folds of the saint's robe were miraculously turned into flowers. Zurbarán chose three species very common in gardens since ancient times. These include the yellow blooms of the wallflower (*Erysimum × cheiri*), a member of the cabbage family that can flower for months at a time, spreading its entrancing scent. There are also a number of fragrant Provence roses (*Rosa × centifolia*), grown since at least the 14th century. Finally, a solitary orange marigold flower adds variety to the garden sprouting from this canvas.

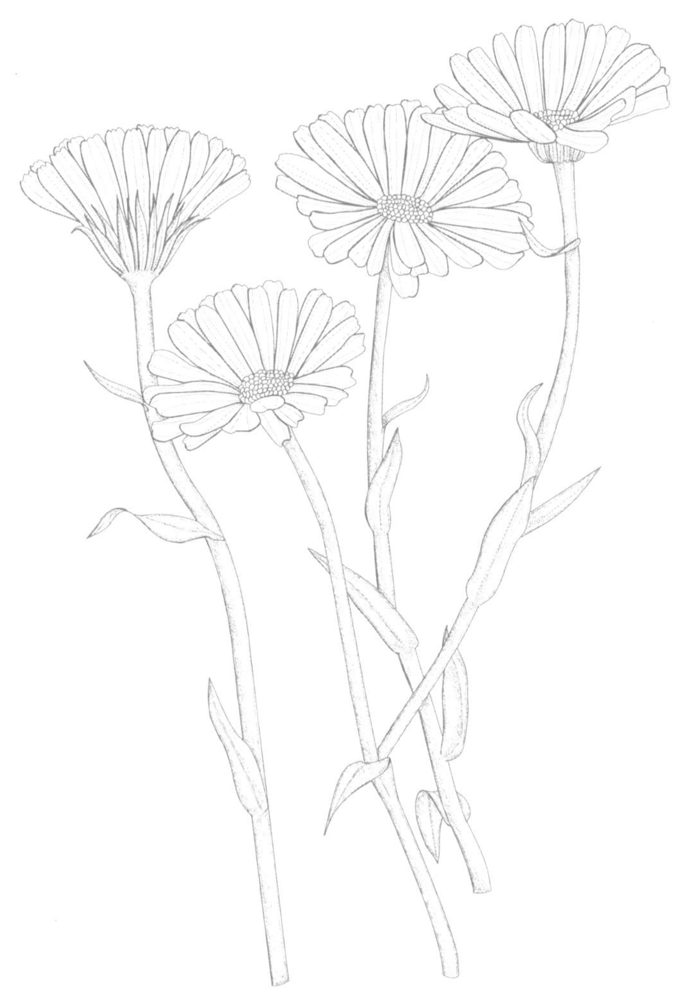

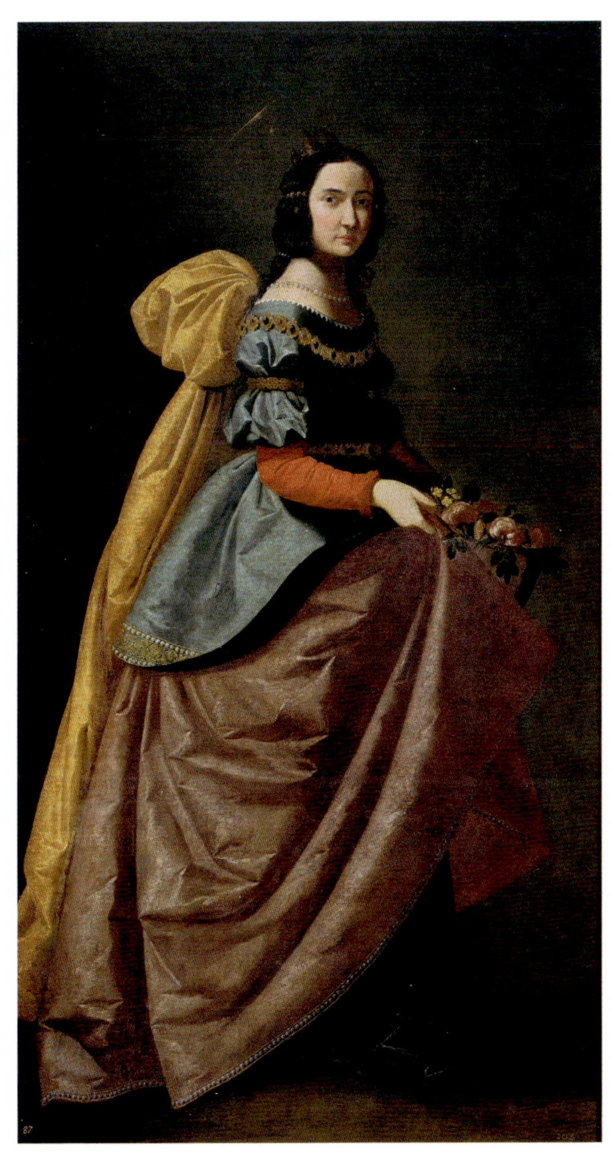

Francisco de Zurbarán
Saint Elisabeth of Portugal
Ca. 1635

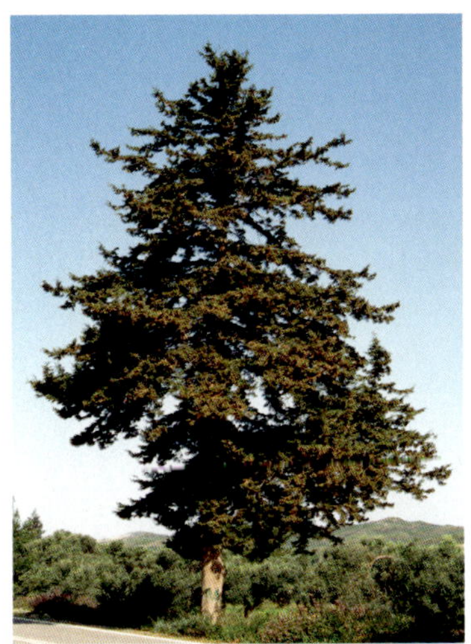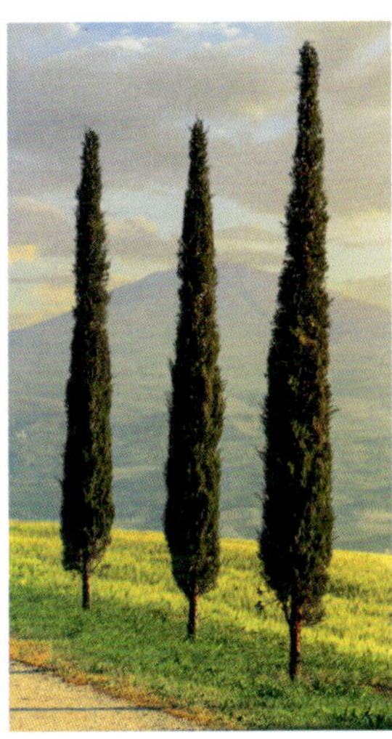

ITALIAN CYPRESS

The cypresses rule over this classical garden, providing a perfect backdrop to the painting with the boarded-up archway. One has a crown with more open, horizontal branches: it is known in Italy as the "female" cypress (*Cupressus sempervirens* f. *horizontalis*), although in fact both sexes are present in the same individual. In contrast, their narrow, column-shaped counterparts are known as "male" cypresses (*Cupressus sempervirens*). In the other painting, a number of cypresses, some of them "female", can be discerned behind the statue of Ariadne.

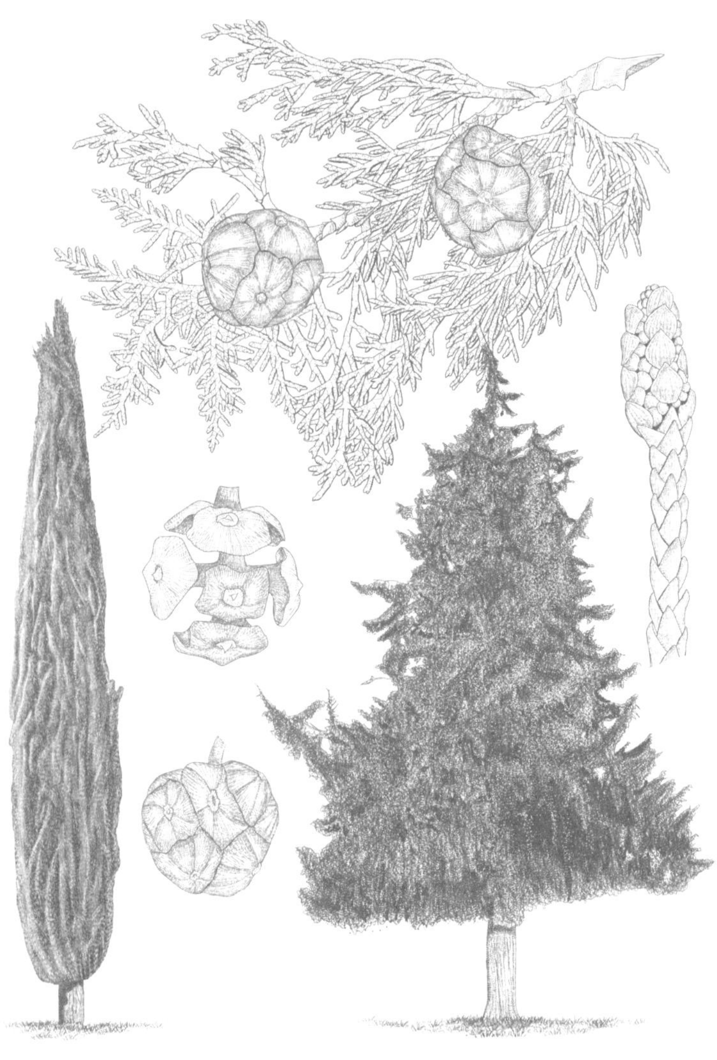

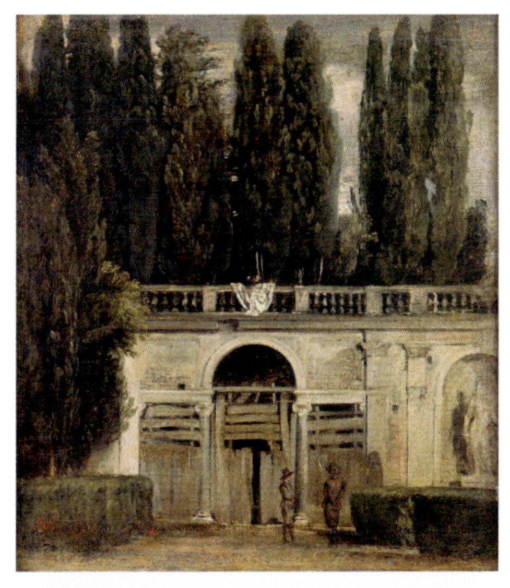

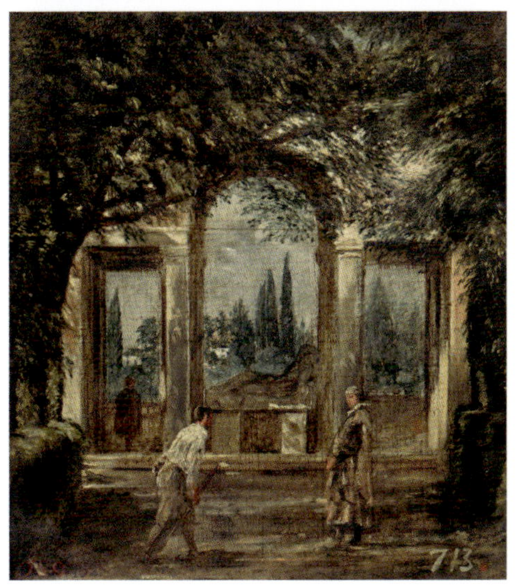

Diego Velázquez
View of the Gardens of the Villa Medici, Rome /
View of the Gardens of the Villa Medici, Rome, with a Statue of Ariadne
Ca. 1630

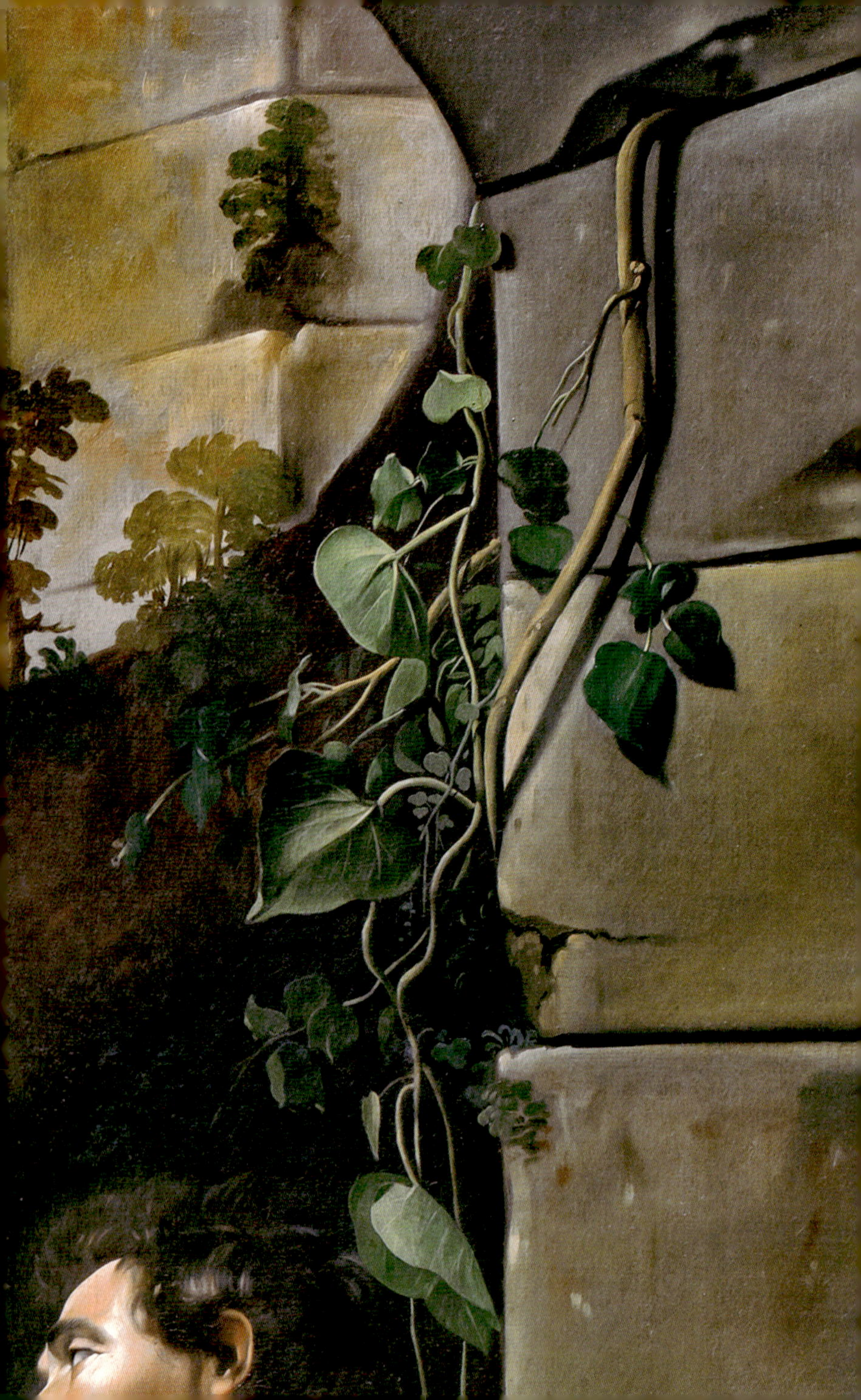

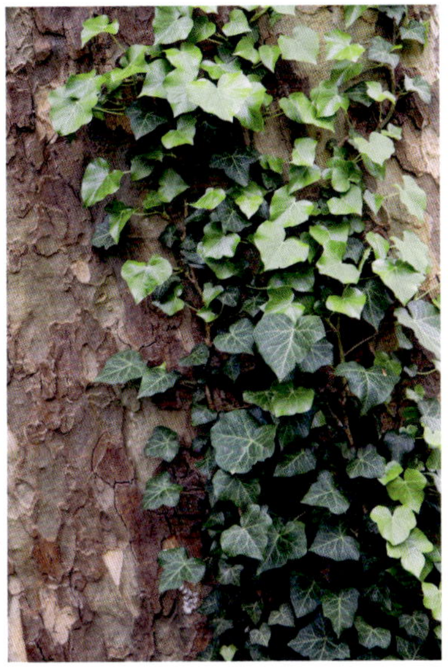

COMMON IVY

If the rose is the most widely-represented plant in the Museo del Prado, with its different species, varieties and cultivars, the single species featured in the largest number of works is ivy. This climbing plant often appears in the background, clinging to a wall or tree. Its forms also adorn classical statues, such as the head of the Roman god Bacchus. In this religious painting, where the artist has focused on the more rounded leaves of its fertile stems, the ivy with its evergreen foliage symbolises eternal life.

Hedera helix

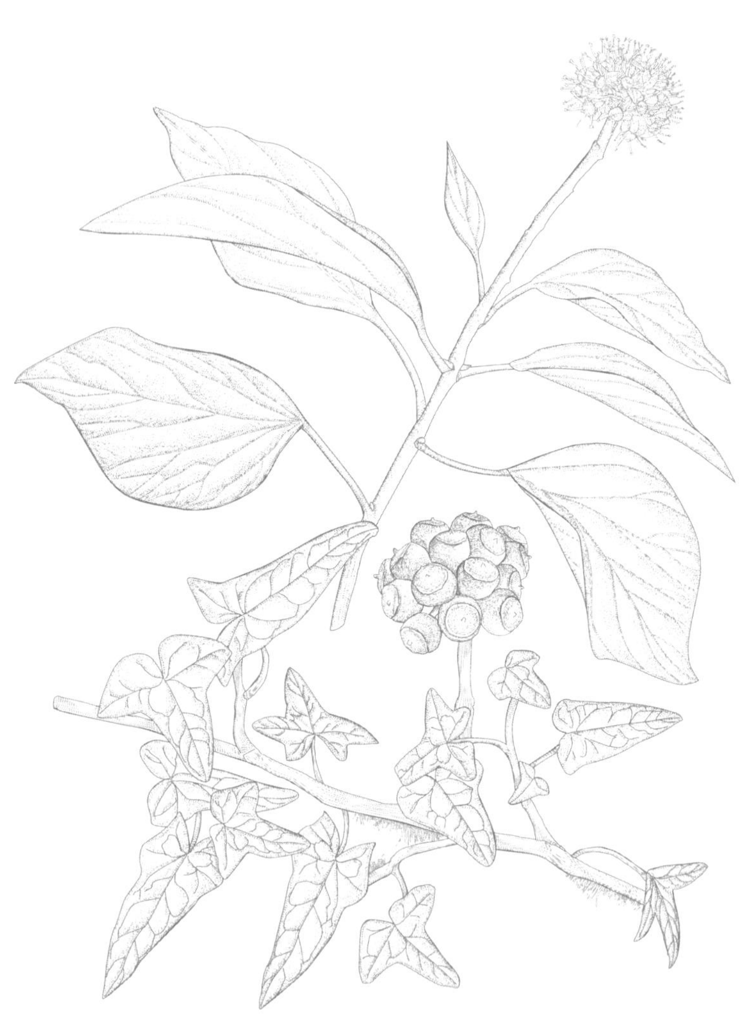

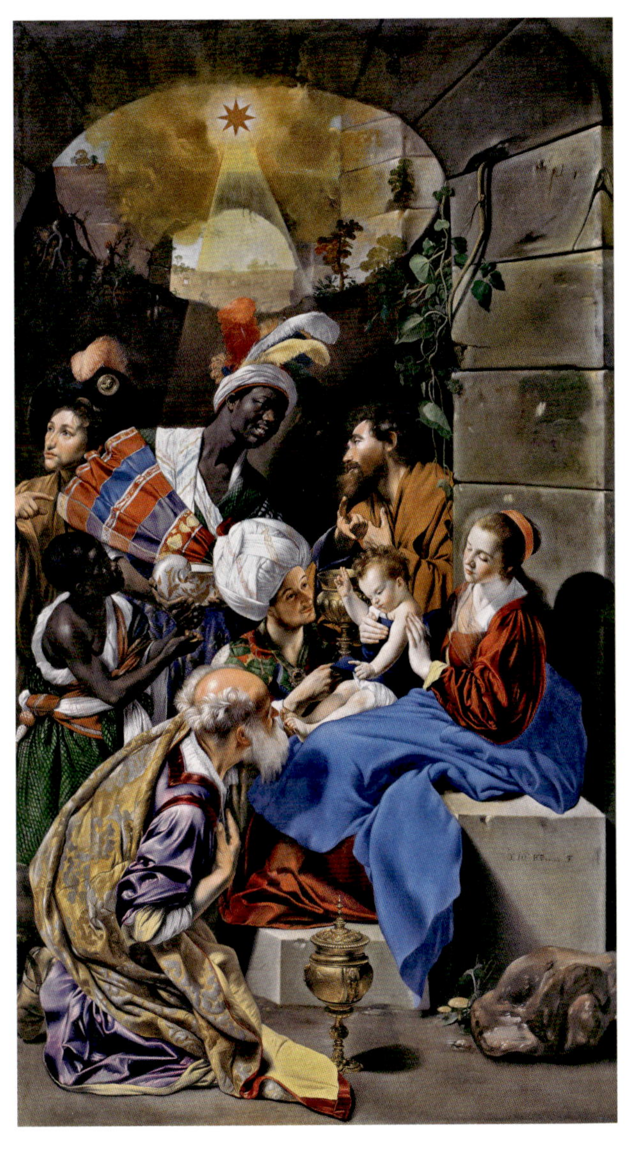

Fray Juan Bautista Maíno
The Adoration of the Magi
1612-1614

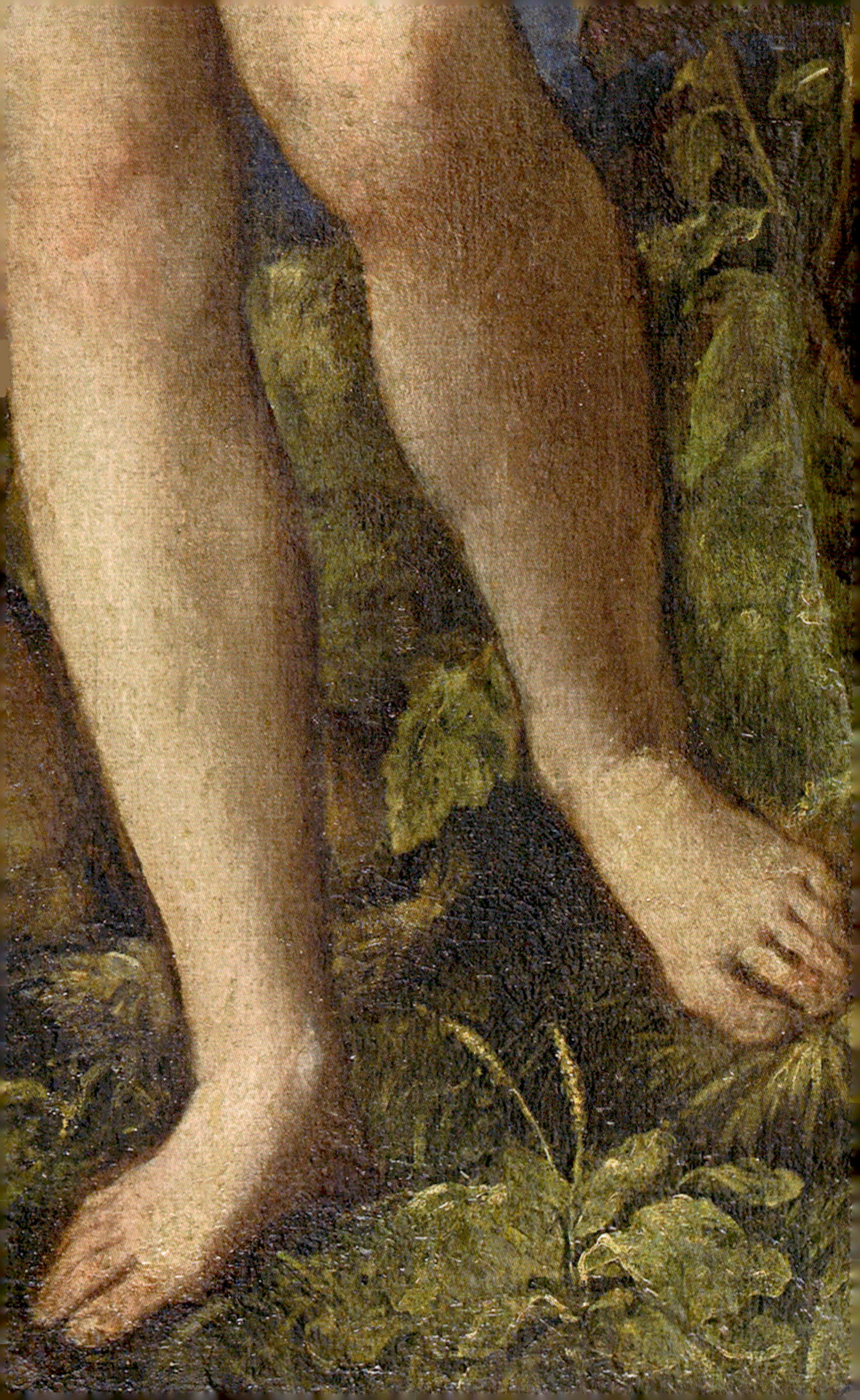

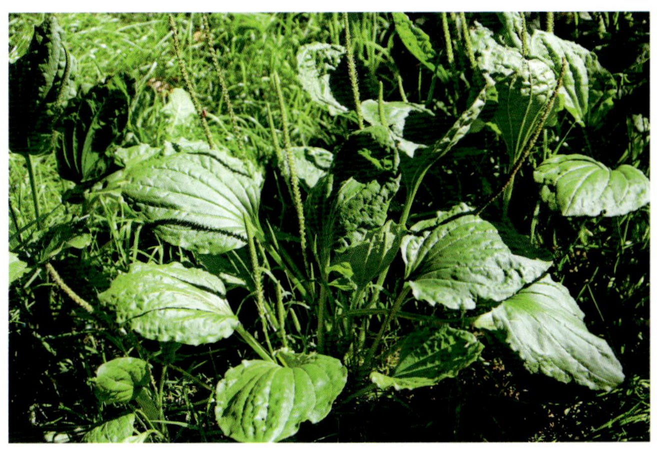

GREATER PLANTAIN

At Eve's feet we can see two greater plantain inflorescences. Because of their slightly spear-like appearance, they have been linked to the martyrdom of Christ. For that reason, plantain is commonly found in Crucifixion scenes. It also embodied the struggle of good against evil, and therefore symbolised salvation. Additionally, because it tends to grow beside footpaths, it was adopted as a metaphor for the path leading to Christ. Since ancient times, its leaves – applied as a poultice – have been used to heal foot wounds after long walks.

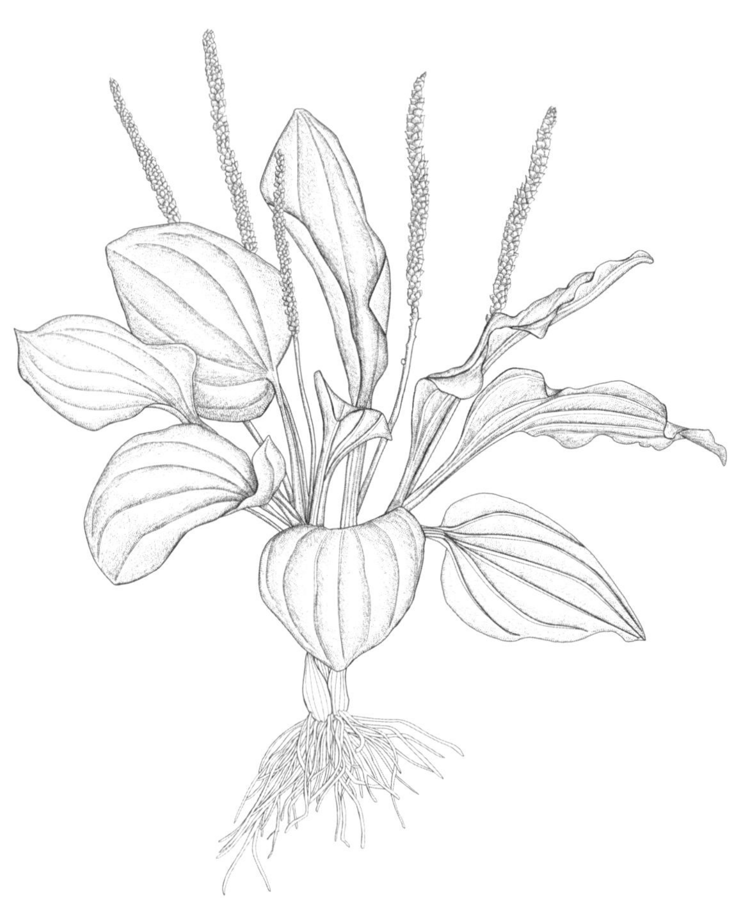

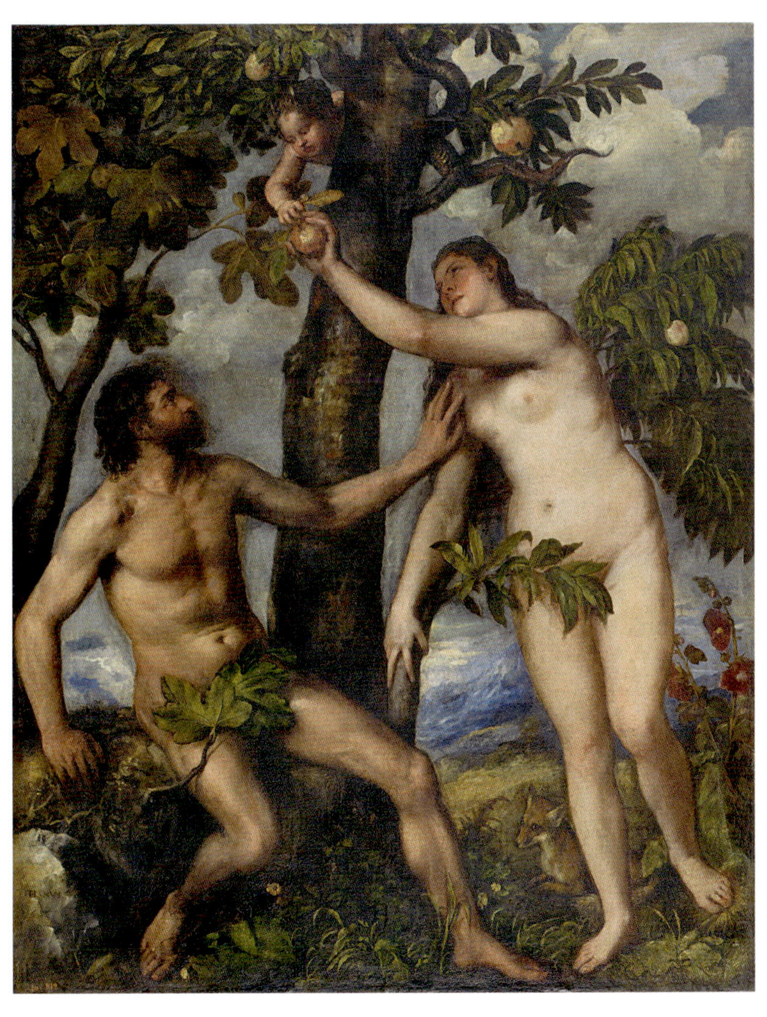

Titian (Tiziano Vecellio)
Adam and Eve
Ca. 1550

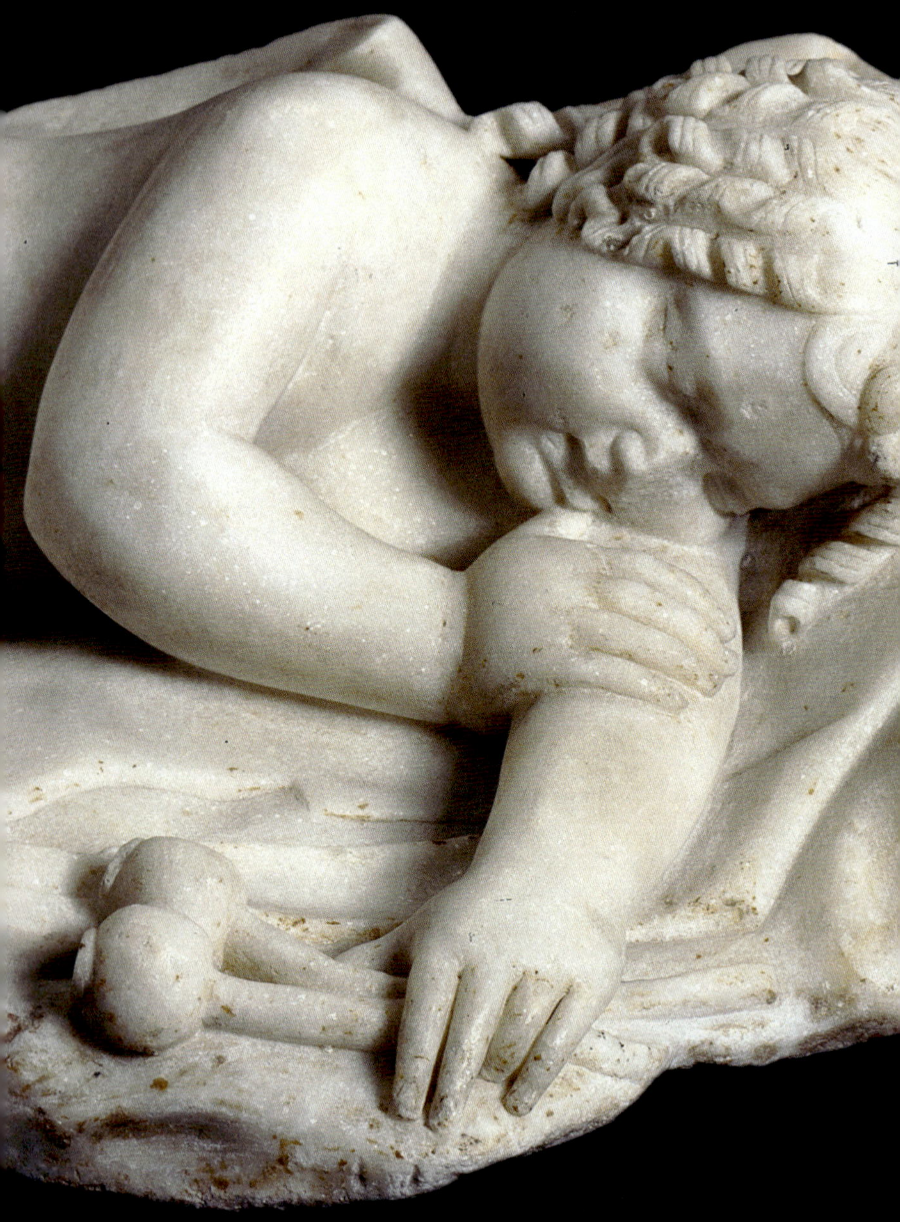

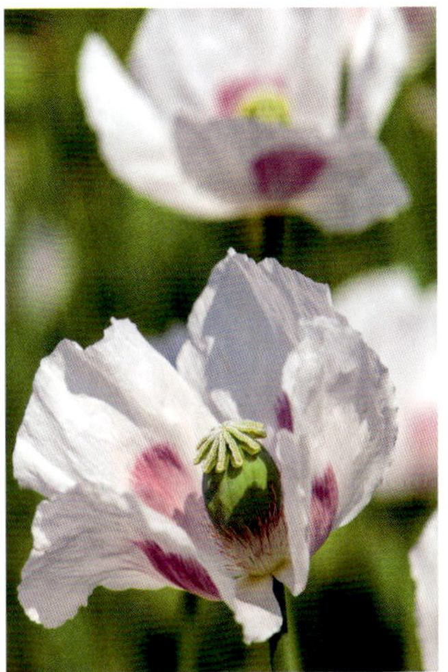 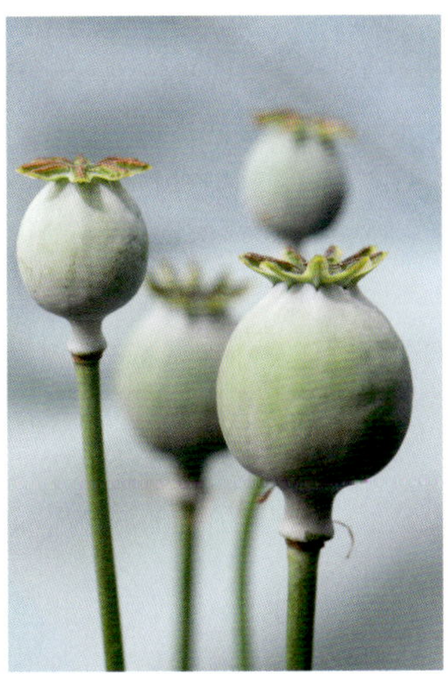

OPIUM POPPY

The opium poppy is linked to a number of Greek deities, among them Hypnos, Morpheus, Cybele, Demeter and Aphrodite. Its medicinal use as a sedative has led to it being used to symbolise sleep. Here the sleeping child lightly holds two poppy fruits, from which opium resin is extracted; derivates obtained from the resin are still used today to alleviate all kinds of physical pain. In ancient Rome, opium was among the ingredients of the famous theriac, an antidote against poisons and certain diseases.

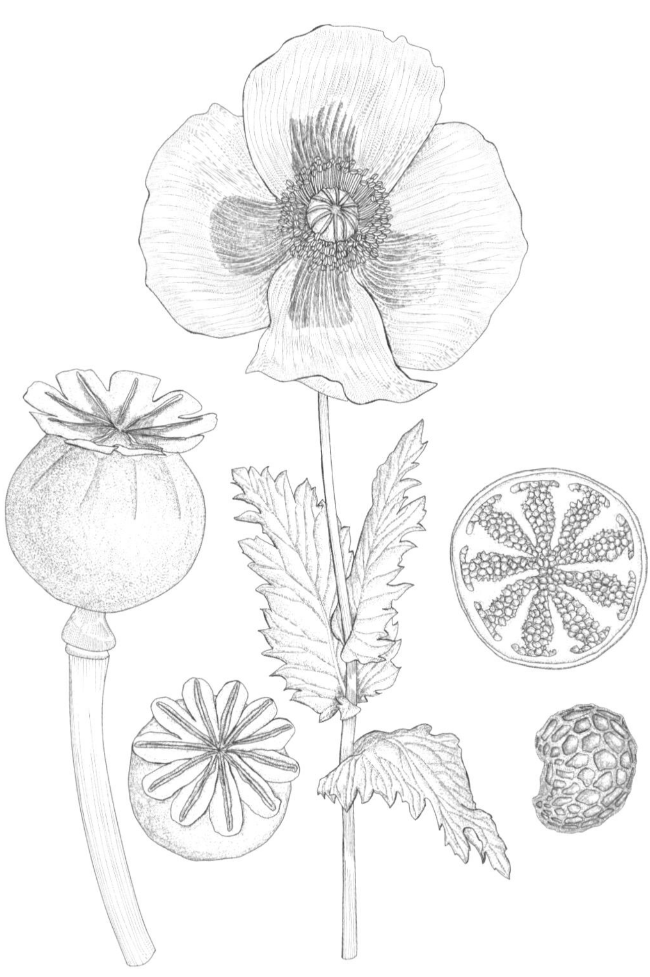

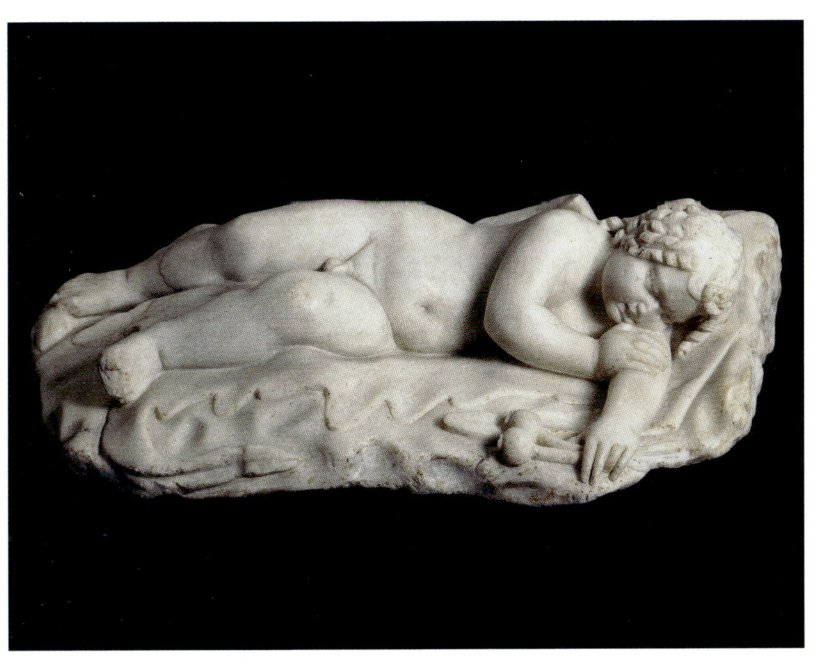

Roman Sculptor
Sleeping Eros or *Hypnos*
100-130

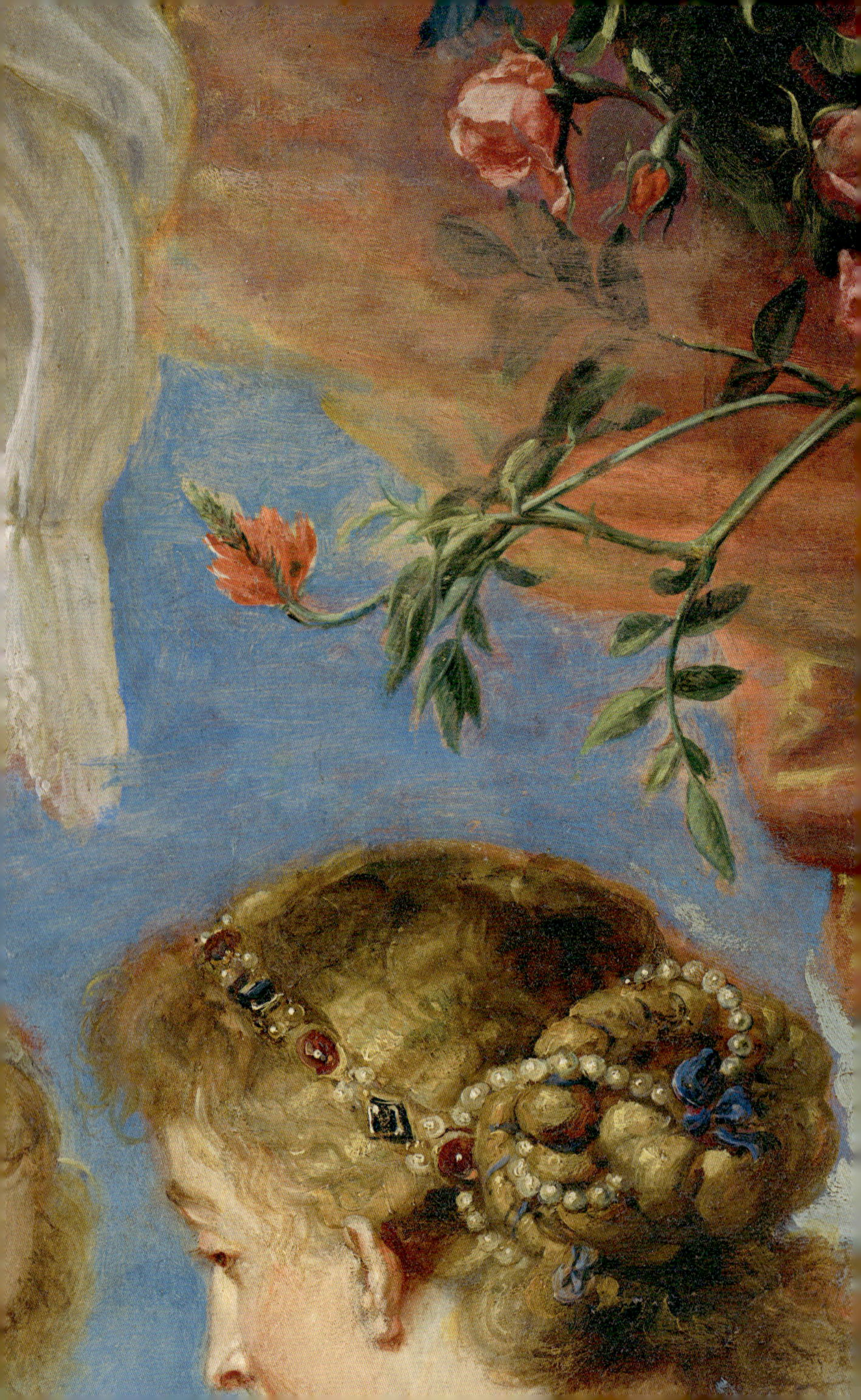

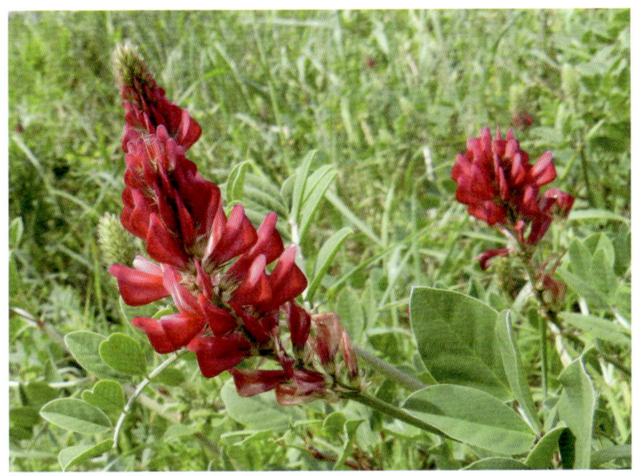

FRENCH HONEYSUCKLE

The three Graces meet under a floral garland, consisting mainly of roses, the symbol of love. Indeed, it may be regarded as a small compendium of the varieties most widely cultivated at that time: 'Maiden's Blush', with its slightly pink tinge; the white rose of York, the Provence rose and the red *Rosa gallica*. Hanging from the garland, a flower is outlined against the blue sky. This is the French honeysuckle, a species not commonly found in works of art, which perhaps had a special significance for Rubens.

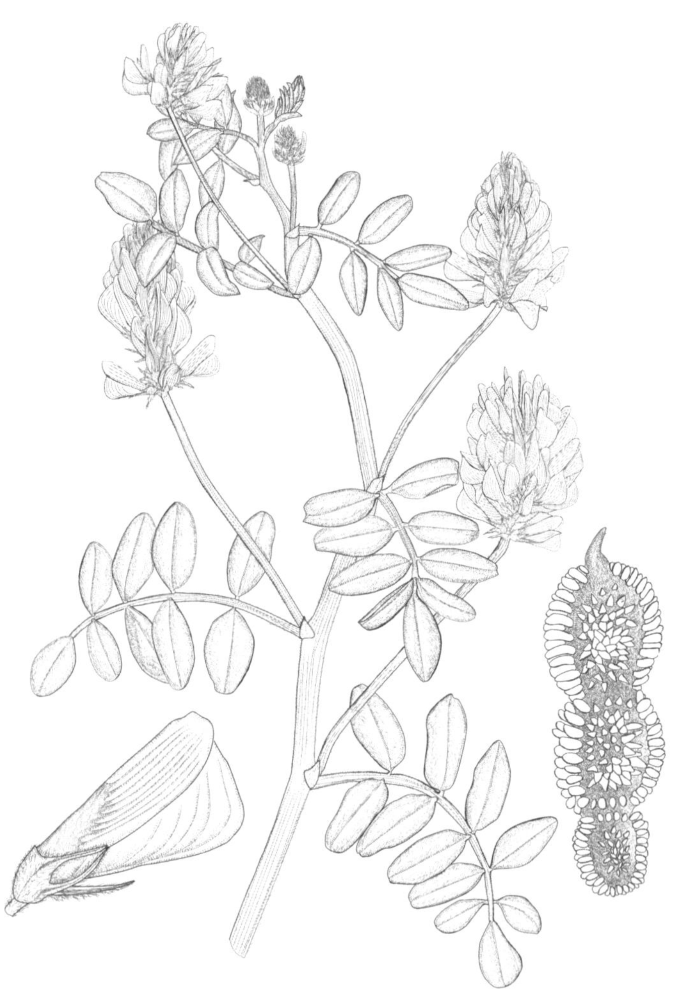

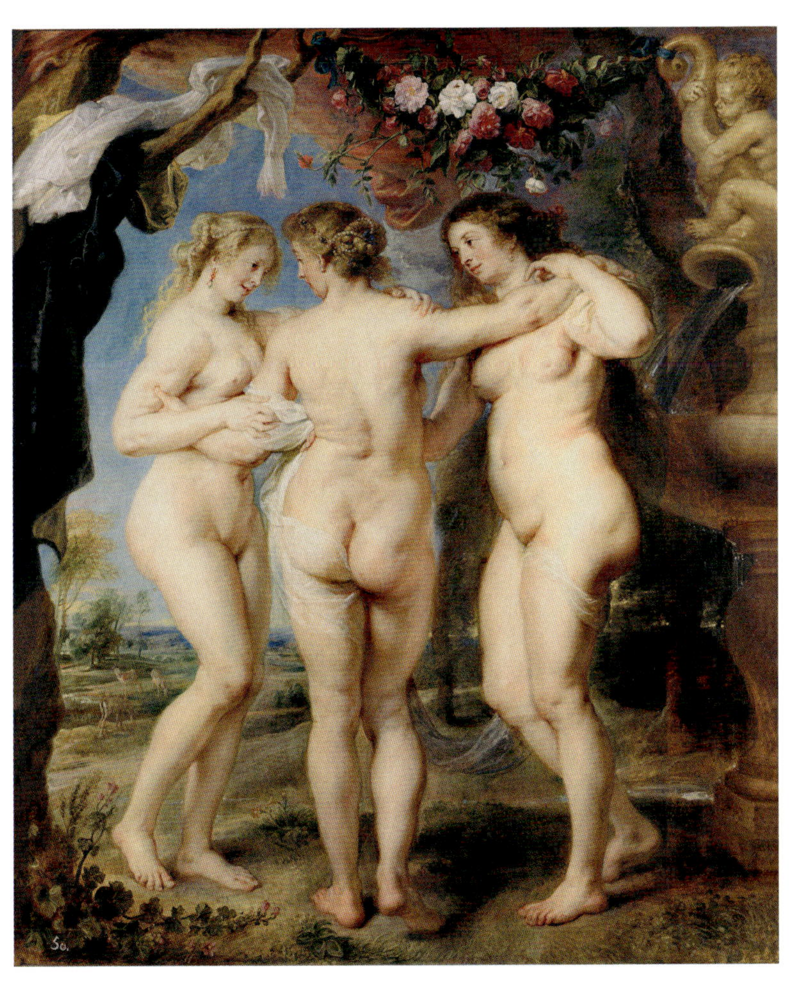

Peter Paul Rubens
The Three Graces
1630-1635

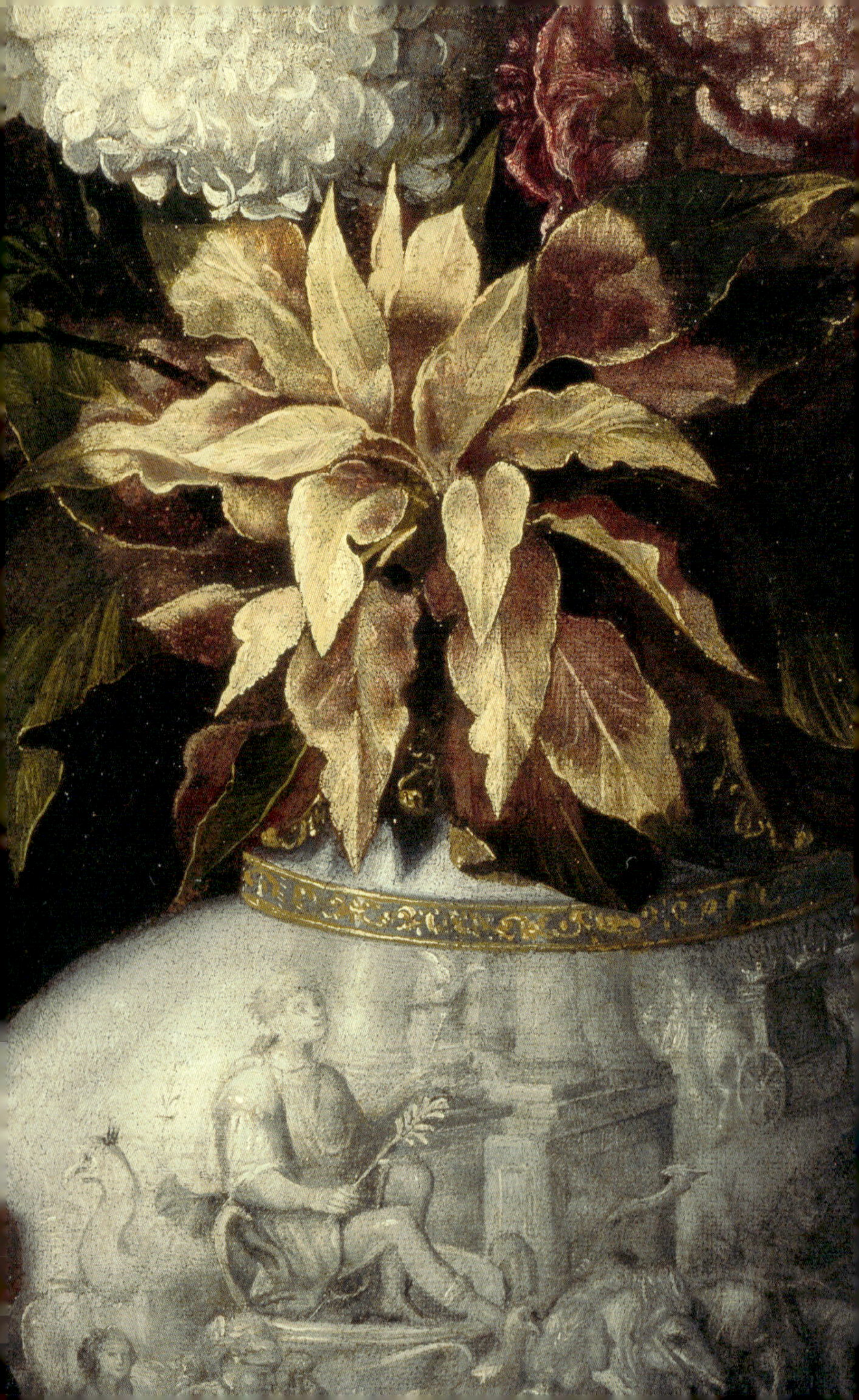

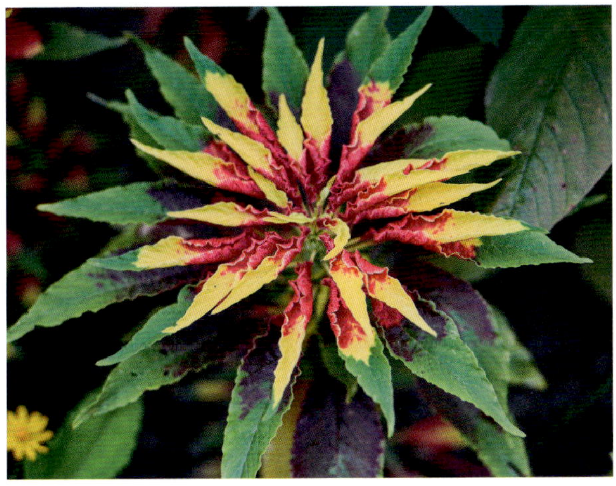

EDIBLE AMARANTH

The history of plants is full of travel. Many of the species we grow today were brought from distant lands. The flowers in this vase include the common poppy (*Papaver rhoeas*), an archaeophyte, i.e. a species which spread as humans colonised new regions, prior to the conquest of America. Its seeds were transported alongside those of crops such as wheat. The painting depicts other plants from far-off places: the sunflower (*Helianthus annuus*), native to America, and the edible amaranth, from Asia.

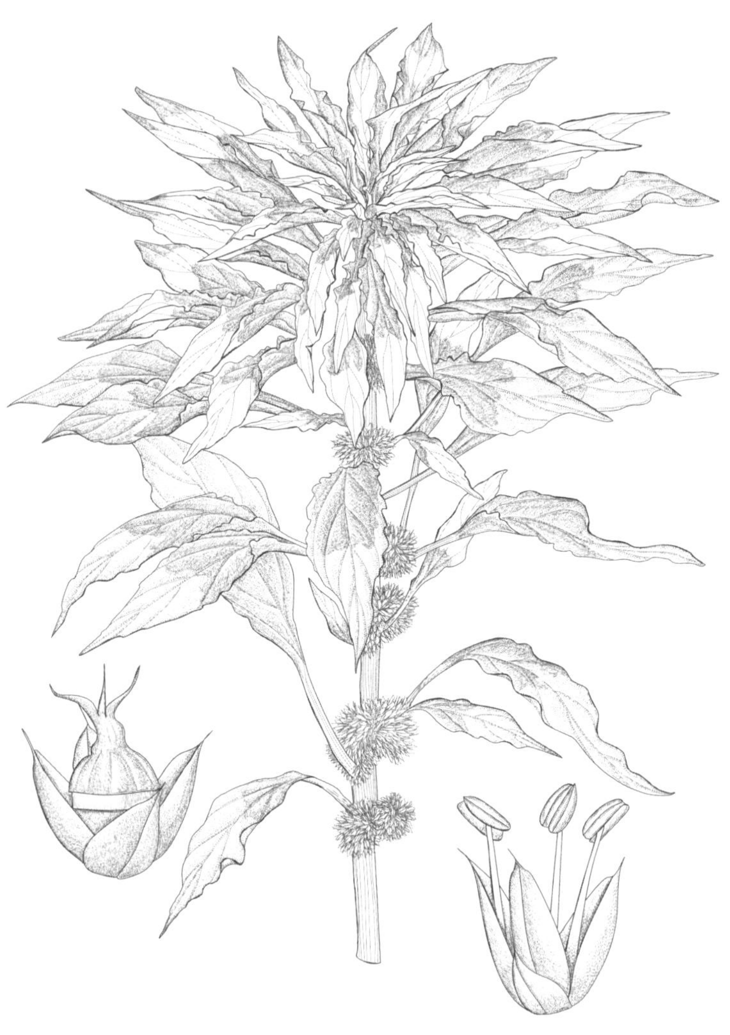

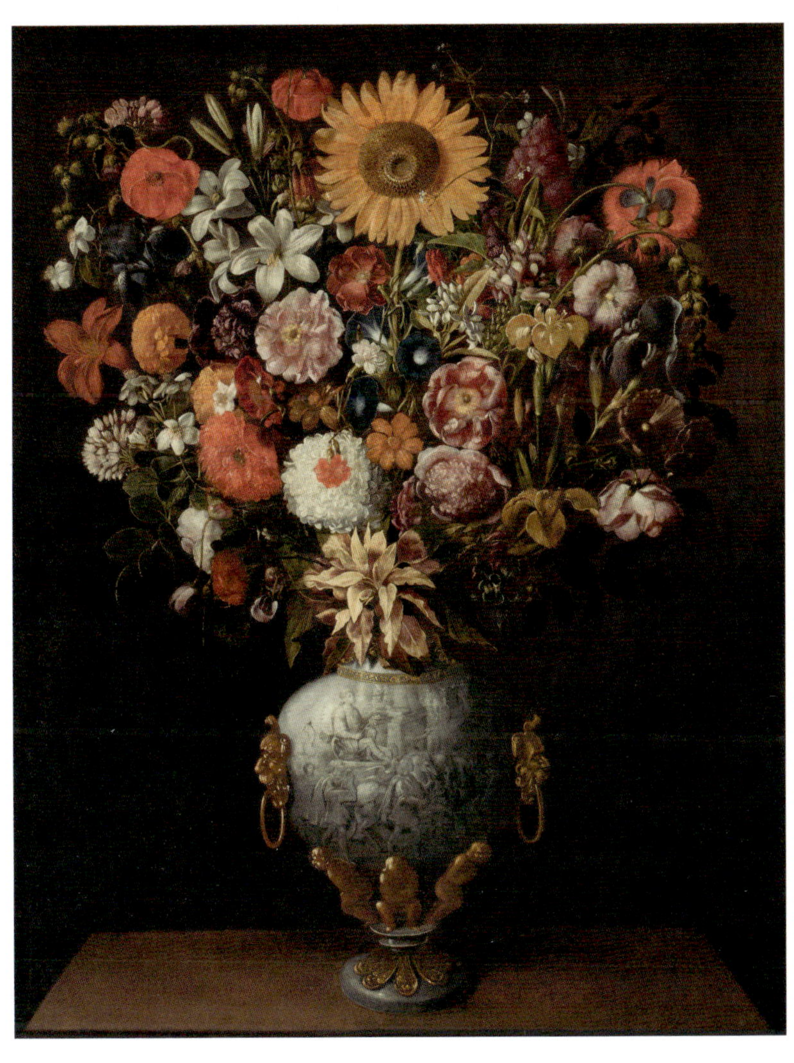

Tomás Hiepes
Vase of Flowers decorated with a Triumphal Chariot seen in Profile
1643

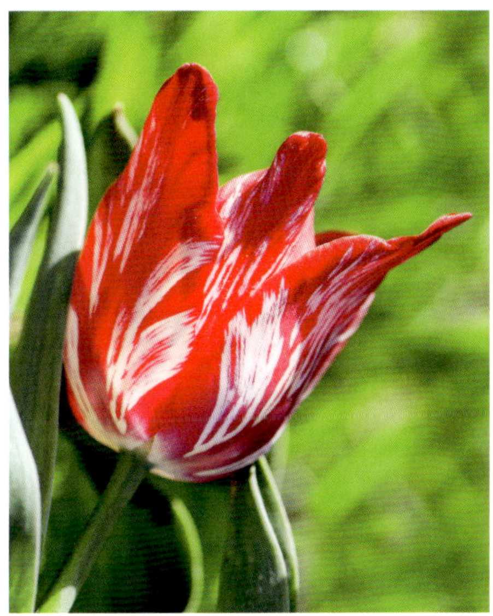

TULIP

Certain flowers predominated in many compositions of the Baroque period. Some of the most common can be found in this still life by Arellano: double-flowered poppy anemones (*Anemone coronaria* cv.), Provence roses (*Rosa* × *centifolia*), bearded irises (*Iris* × *germanica*) and carnations (*Dianthus caryophyllus*). Another widely-depicted flower was the tulip, a single example of which appears here, its tepals tinted red and white. These two-colour forms, whose tonal patterns are caused by the tulip breaking virus, are known as broken or variegated tulips.

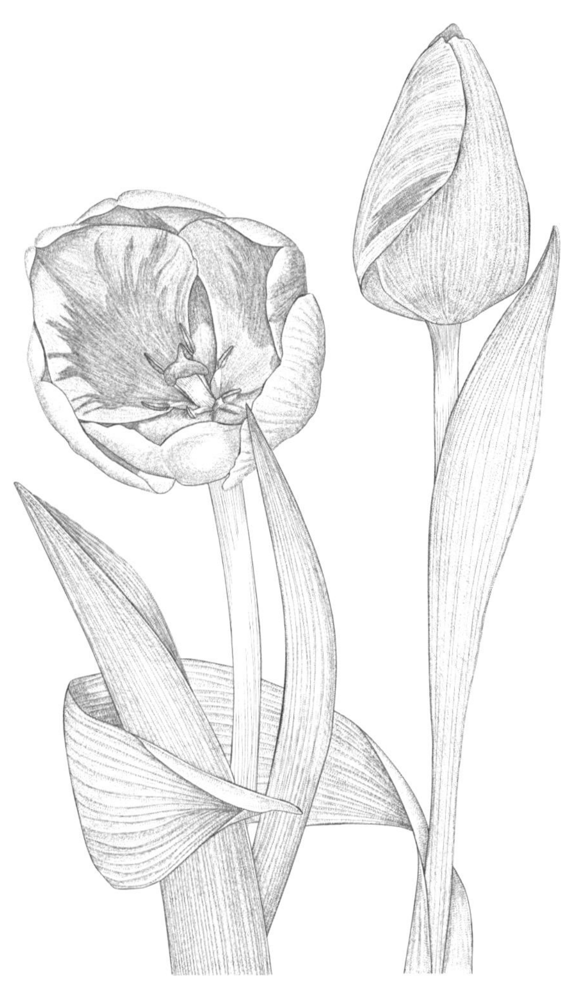

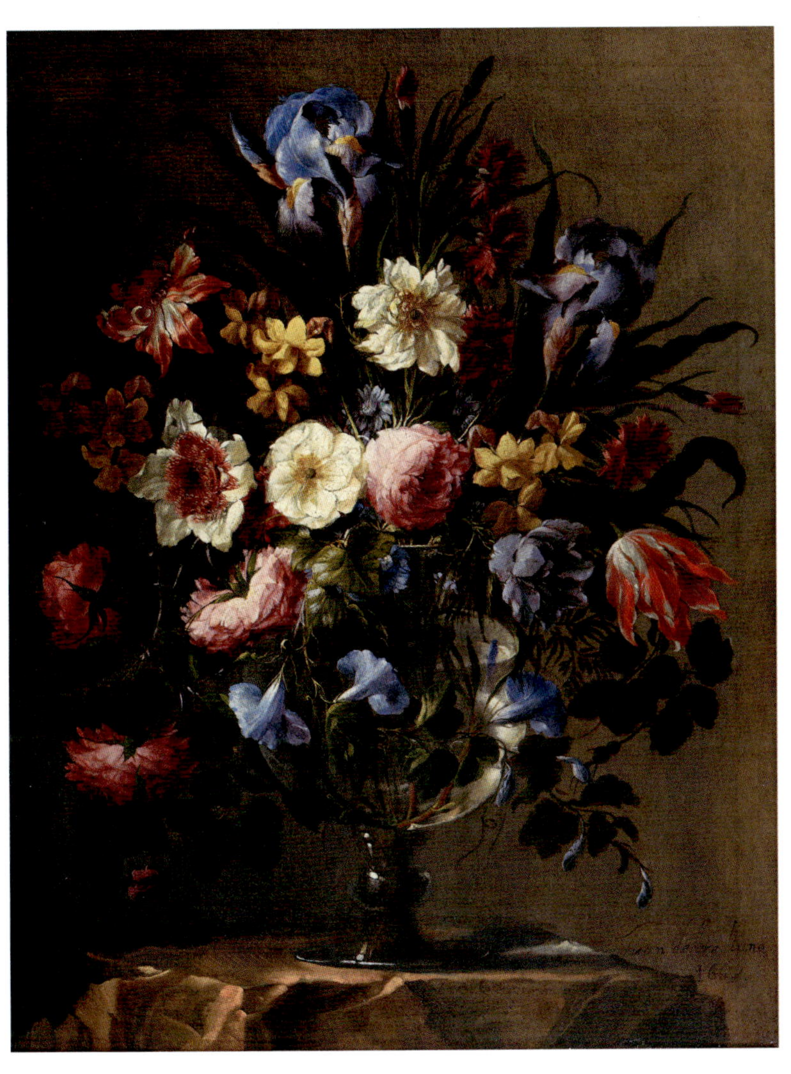

Juan de Arellano
Flowers in a Glass Vase
1668

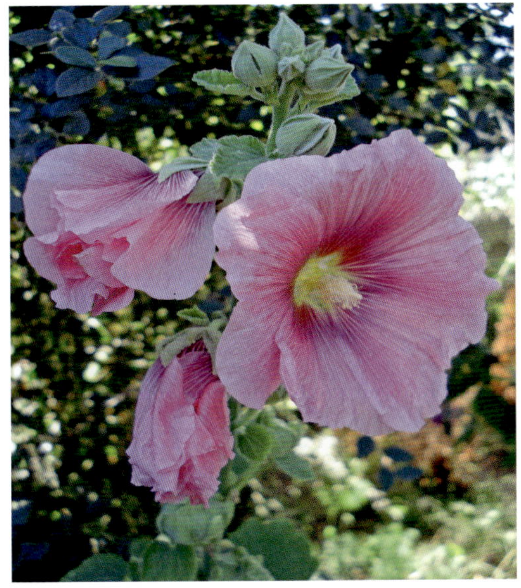

COMMON HOLLYHOCK

The cypresses (*Cupressus sempervirens*) in the background of this garden recall those painted by Velázquez at the Villa Medici. A family is gathered at the entrance of the house, in a grapevine bower (*Vitis vinifera*). A number of hollyhocks have been planted beside the door, a practice still common today. They are quite tall, and dotted with flowers, many of which are pink. Hollyhocks were used to cure snakebites and scorpion stings, and are therefore regarded as beneficial.

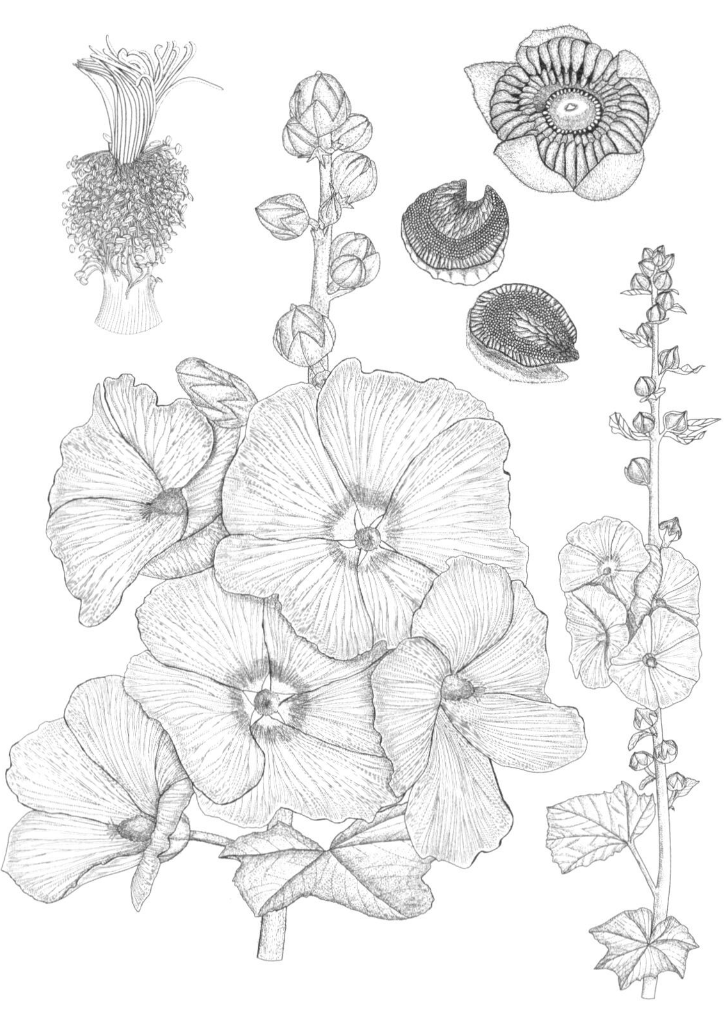

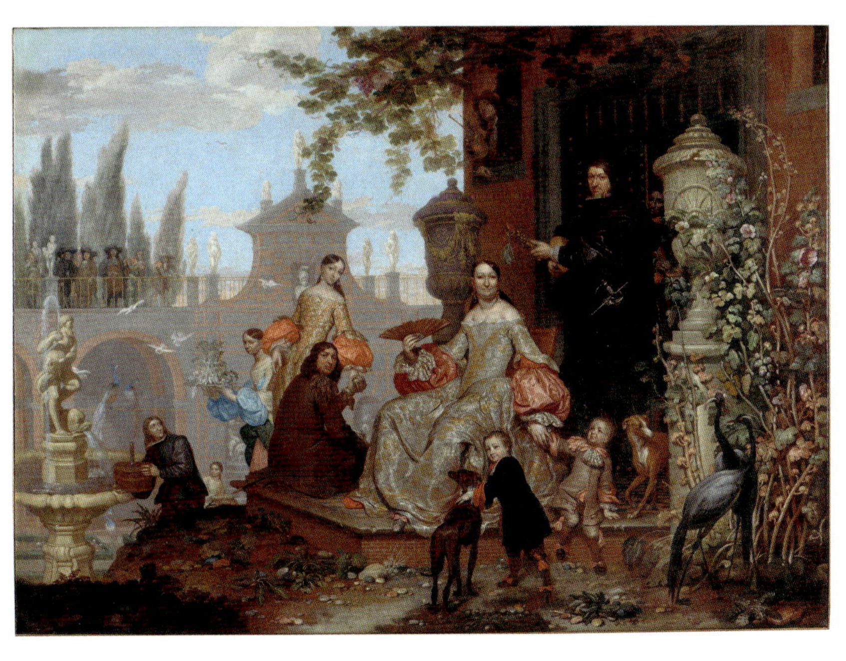

Jan van Kessel the Younger
Family in a Garden
1679

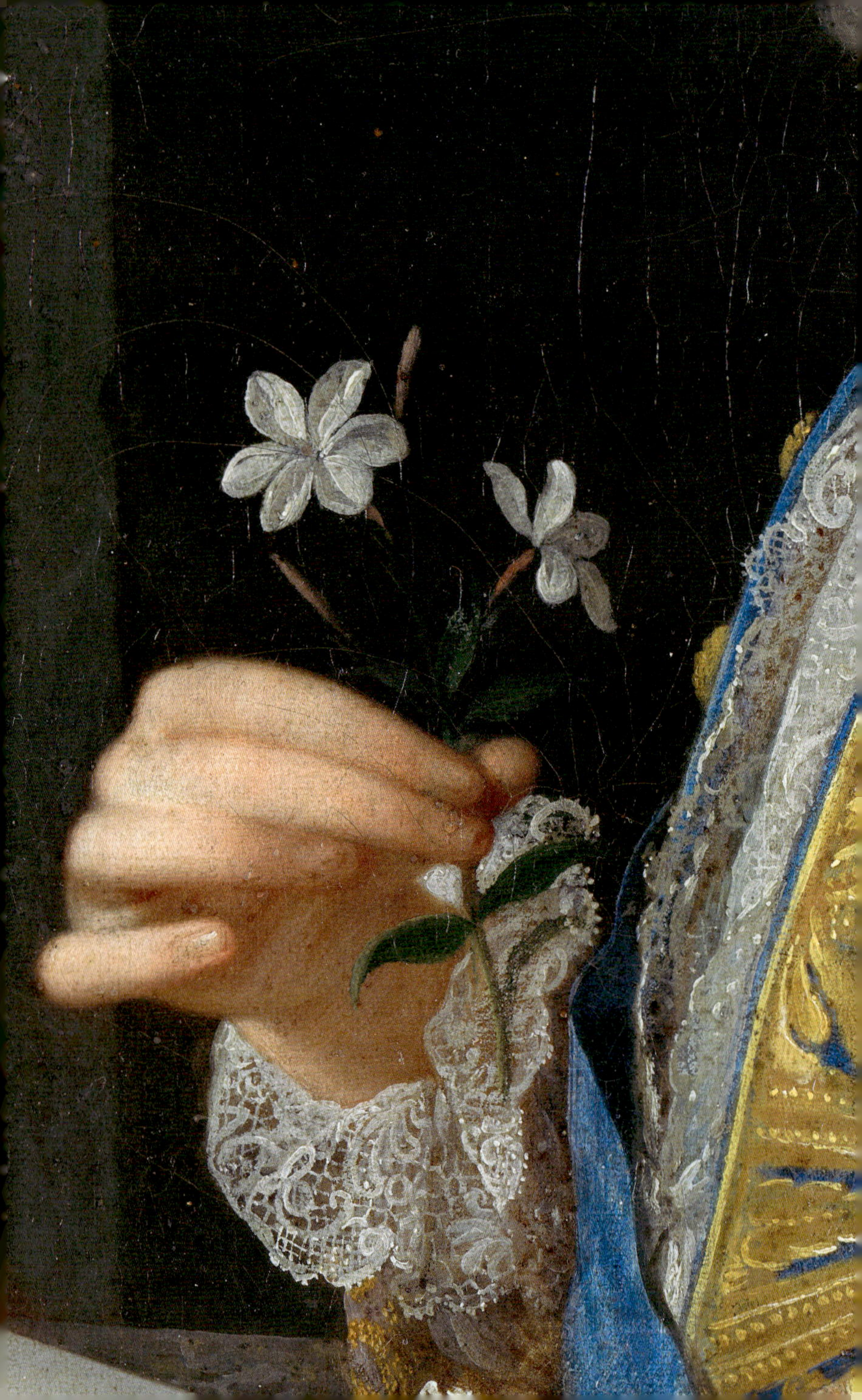

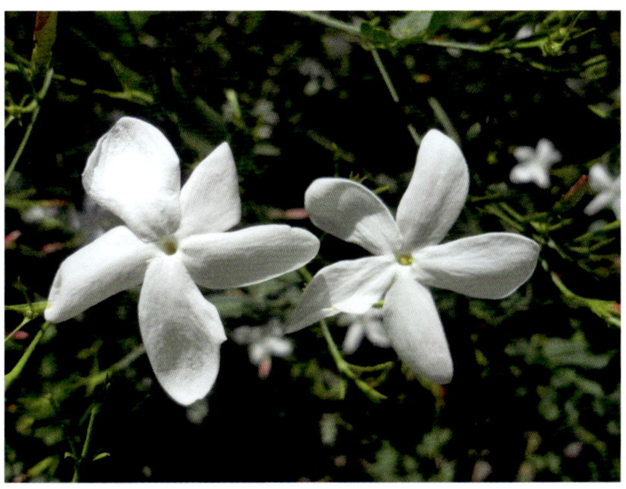

SPANISH JASMINE

The large vase on the table contains a veritable garden of cut flowers. The upper part is crowned by an English iris (*Iris latifolia*), a plant native to the Pyrenees and the Cantabrian Mountains. Below this special flower, others are placed in a harmonious arrangement, in the same tones as the prince's clothing. The Spanish jasmine he is holding is remarkable in that it has six petals, rather than the usual five. Perhaps the prince is keen to display this rare find, as was customary in cabinets of curiosities.

Jasminum grandiflorum

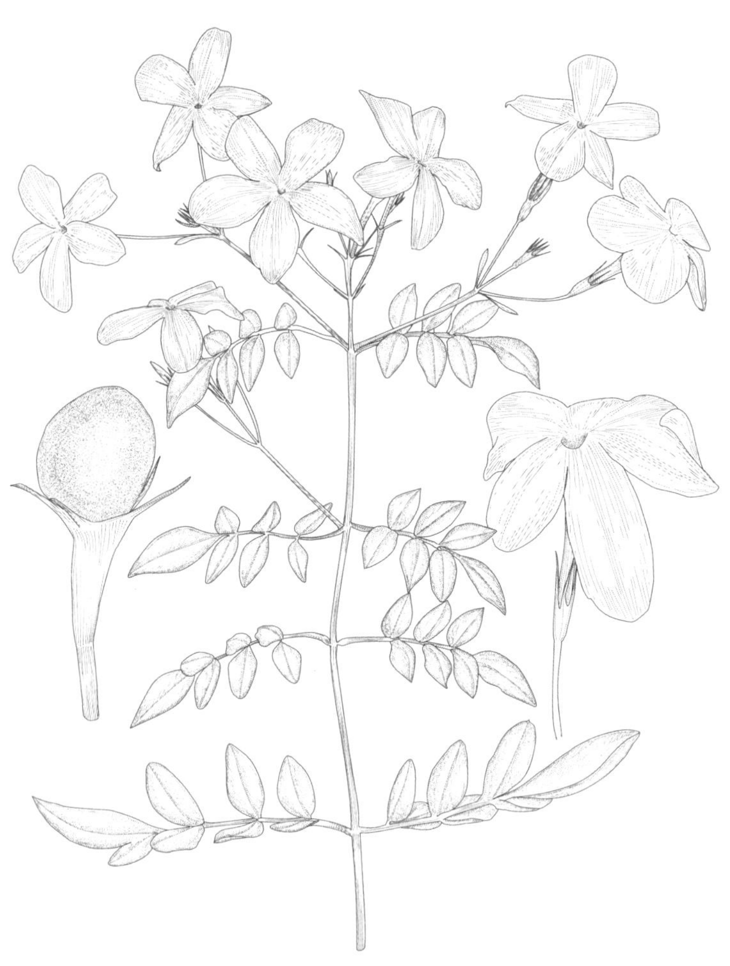

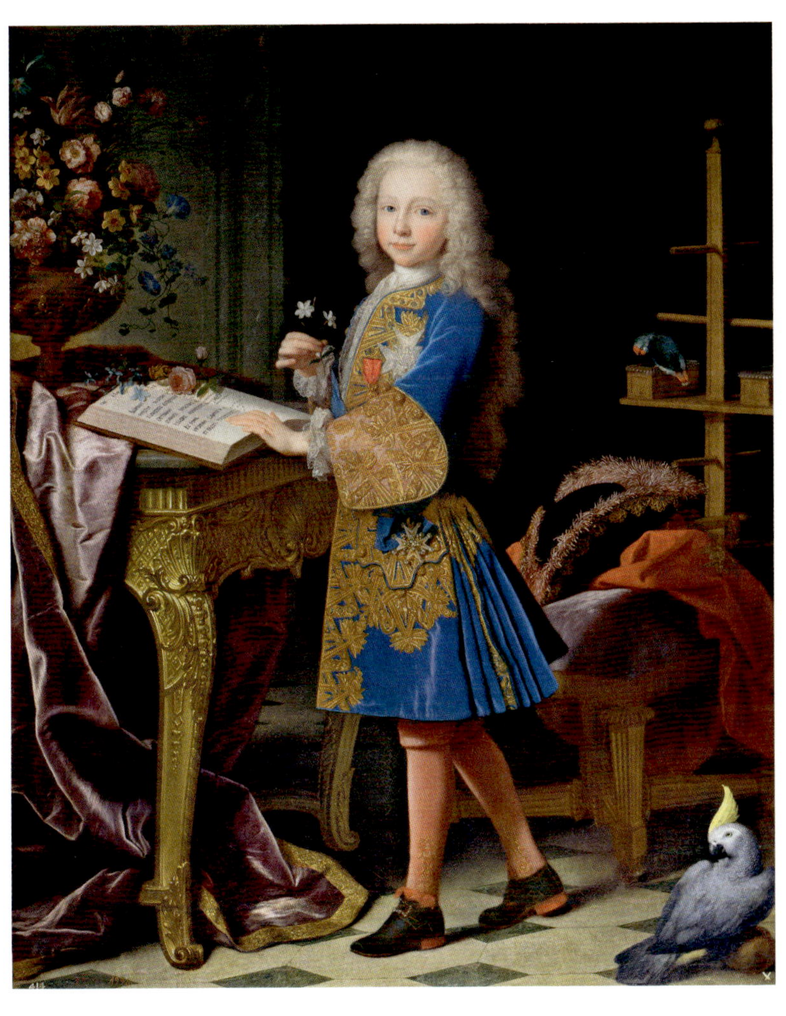

Jean Ranc
Charles III as a Boy in his Study
Ca. 1724

Index of Species

Index of Authors and Works

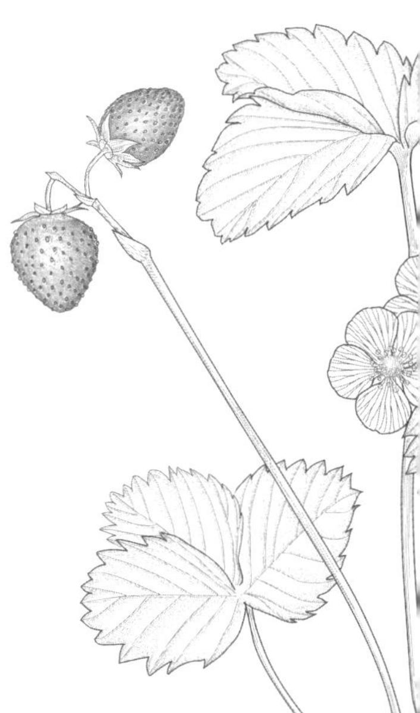

Published by Museo Nacional del
Prado Difusión on the occasion of the
itinerary *A Botanical Stroll Through the
Prado* (29 October 2024 – 30 March
2025, Museo Nacional del Prado,
Madrid).

CURATOR AND AUTHOR OF THE TEXTS
Eduardo Barba Gómez

COORDINATION AND EDITION
Museo Nacional del Prado Difusión
Production Department

DESIGN AND LAYOUT
Fernando Gutiérrez Studio

TRANSLATOR
Paul Edson

PHOTOGRAPHIC DOCUMENTATION
Eduardo Barba Gómez, Michele Leong

SCIENTIFIC ILLUSTRATIONS
Juan Luis Castillo

PREPRESS
Lucam

PRINTING AND BINDING
Estudios Gráficos Europeos, S.A.

PRINTED IN SPAIN

© This edition: Museo Nacional del Prado
Difusión, 2024

ISBN: 978-84-8480-624-0
NIPO: 195-24-039-4
DL: M-20105-2024

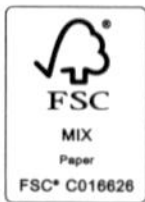

Museo del Prado publications catalogue:
www.tiendaprado.com